ART OF THE FORMAL GARDEN

ART OF THE FORMAL GARDEN

 AREND JAN VAN DER HORST

PHOTOGRAPHED BY
BRIGITTE AND PHILIPPE PERDEREAU

CASSELL

Photograph on endpapers:
Manoir d'Eyrignac, Dordogne.

Photograph facing title page:
*Dark lines cut across the gravel at Cobblers
Garden in Crowborough, East Sussex.*

Photograph on title page:
*Imaginative symmetry created by Willem
Bursens, Gent, with* Achillea *and grey-leafed*
Santolina *by a romantic white gate.*

Photograph on pages 6/7:
*These tapered and neatly clipped hedges
act as stage wings between two sections of
a garden.*

This edition first published in the UK 1995 by
Cassell
Wellington House
125 Strand
London
WC2R 0BB

Volume copyright
© Terra Publishing Co., Warnsveld 1994
Text copyright
© Avend Jan van der Horst 1994
English translation copyright
© Cassell 1995
Translation: Mary Charles, in association
with First Edition Translations Ltd

Distributed in the United States by
Sterling Publishing Co. Inc.
387 Park Avenue South
New York, NY 10016 USA

Distributed in Australia by Capricorn Link (Australia) Pty Ltd
2/13 Carrington Road, Castle Hill, NSW 2154

British Library Cataloguing-in-Publication Data
A catalogue record for this book is available from the British Library

ISBN 0-304-347426

Typeset in Great Britain

Contents

Introduction

One hot Saturday afternoon some eighteen years ago, I strolled into the garden at Walenburg, a small castle in the Netherlands. I suddenly found myself amidst a fine selection of perennials and a profusion of scented roses in old-world, delicate shades of pink, white and lilac. What at first seemed like extravagant if delightful chaos, on closer inspection turned out to be a well-designed complex of symmetrical divisions. The superabundance of plants and flowers was enclosed in a formal pattern of hedges, paths and vistas, which was always repeated on the opposite side of the central axis.

That was how I rediscovered symmetry as a framework for gardens within which an exuberance of plants could thrive and flower magnificently. It made me realize that the asymmetry of what was then called 'modern' garden design no longer had to be regarded as the universal solution for every kind of plot. The symmetrical gardens of the medieval, renaissance and baroque periods suddenly appeared to be feasible again, provided the planting was romantic.

I designed my first symmetrical gardens for clients with some trepidation. It soon became obvious that the sun's semi-circular course created different shadows for each hour of the day, so that the light cast on the two identical halves of any one section was hardly ever the same. Light transforms anything that might otherwise seem boringly uniform.

I discovered that Sissinghurst, Hidcote Manor and many other twentieth-century English gardens told the same story. There, too, symmetry turned out to be imaginative and surprisingly inspiring, with perennials, roses, climbers and annuals planted freely within identical divisions.

Brigitte Thomas and Philippe Perdereau, who took the photographs for this book, found out how owners and designers of gardens managed to tackle this phenomenon. They discovered a great many places, hitherto obscure, that may inspire us. The designs added to each chapter show how symmetry in gardens that I had designed achieved functional results. The photographs and designs are independent of one another. They constitute two views of a single phenomenon: imaginative symmetry which, as I know, formed the basis of garden design for many centuries.

Once you have been convinced that symmetry is a good starting-point for romantic gardening, all you need do is enjoy yourself. If you still need to get used to the idea, you should observe how the photographs and designs in this book reveal a constant search for contrasts. Formality and informality, severity and airiness are juxtaposed in a way that only adds to their appeal.

It is therefore my firm belief that imaginative symmetry can offer the very best of all worlds!

*These green yew-tree sentinels guard the
terraces belonging to the house; beyond
them, 'nature' can display its gentle forms.*

Hedges

One of the earliest ways of enclosing gardens was by means of hedges. It is for a very good reason that the original Dutch word *tune*, like its English derivative 'town', means 'fenced-in area'. The elementary idea of pruning plants and allowing them to grow into a dense, scarcely penetrable mass has had enormous consequences in many countries. Clipped hedges in gardens also created an ideal transition from architecture to nature.

In the oldest illustrations of gardens, we often find that walls of wood or stone were used to enclose or subdivide a particular area. The same effect could be achieved with clipped plants. Rows of plants forming dense walls of vegetation were equally satisfactory for subdividing space and for enclosing gardens. It is obvious that a hedge will be less effective than a stone wall for sealing off a garden against undesirable intruders. Regular pruning, however, or plants with thorns or prickly leaves such as hawthorn or holly, can achieve a more impervious and impenetrable effect.

It was a logical development that these green walls were used not only for functional purposes, but also because of their beauty. Their purpose in gardens has changed over the centuries, but the basic principles have remained largely the same.

Anyone looking at old gardening books and historical illustrations will find that some garden layouts have remained popular for hundreds of years. Symmetrical gardens in particular have always appealed to their owners, even in periods when asymmetrical design reigned supreme. Vegetable and cut-flower gardens retained their symmetrical divisions with high brick walls or severely clipped hedges concealing them from the view of visitors to parks or gardens.

The beech (Fagus sylvatica) hedge shows visitors where the private garden of the two owners begins. This cobbled path edged with the kind of plants traditionally grown in the gardens of country houses in the northern Netherlands is situated at the entrance to the garden belonging to the Garden Gallery at Eext, in the Dutch province of Drenthe.

Symmetry with hedges

The widely disseminated sixteenth-century book by Hans Vredeman de Vries is one of the earliest publications (1583) on garden design. It contains illustrations of gardens designed in the Italian style, which could be copied by the owners of large or small gardens in the Low Countries.

Many of these Italian examples – the gardens of the Villa Lante, Palazzo Farnese (Caprarola), Villa d'Este and Villa della Petraia – have survived. They are all sixteenth and early-seventeenth-century renaissance gardens and show that a symmetrical layout was a generally accepted way of subdividing space at the time. Yet these gardens are

Straight and curved hedges are separated and linked by the sharp-edged linearity of the perennials. (Jardin d'Eyrignac, Dordogne.)

Beech (Fagus sylvatica) in the wintry sunshine in the garden of landscape architect André van Wassenhoven at Damme (near Bruges).

often highly original because their owners, the clients, and the architects advising them, Da Vignola for instance, managed to add a personal sparkle to the designs. They used perspective to make an area look exciting. Hedges, statuary, walls, shrubs and trees as well as potted plants were employed to subdivide the space and create a succession of individually interesting areas out of a single large plot.

The stone statuary, walls and pots are often all that remains, but old illustrations also show the hedges subdividing the garden. Sometimes the hedges have been replanted, as at the Villa Lante. Usually, however, they have disappeared and we have to use our imagination to recreate the layout.

Even before Vredeman de Vries, books published by such French designers as Jacques du Cerceau (1559/1565), gave examples of 'royal' gardens with severely symmetrical layouts. Even the flower beds were square, so that the whole garden was subdivided according to a geometrical design.

In the seventeenth century, designs by Claude Mollet and his son André replaced the multiplicity of small divisions by a single large one which was to play an important role as a component of the baroque parterres. Four large divisions were frequently created, as may be seen in the lower garden of the Dutch palace Het Loo. They were sometimes surrounded by a border of flowers and small clipped yew, cypress,

Flowering shrubs behind beech crenellations, with landscape architect Jacques Wirtz' perennials at Izegem displaying their variety of colours between box hedges.

I designed arches of climbing fruit trees over the pathway surrounding Pieter Baak's and Frank Linschoten's herb garden with its edgings of clipped herbs. (Garden Gallery at Eext in the Dutch province of Drenthe.)

holly or juniper trees. The centre was usually filled with grass. André le Nôtre took over this idea and embellished the parterres with stone chippings and small clipped trees including box. Claude Mollet was in fact the first designer to use box when he created the small evergreen hedges for the parterres in the gardens of the French king Henri IV. Severe winters made it impossible to grow cypress hedges since they could not withstand extreme cold and needed frequent replacing. For that reason the royal gardener Claude Mollet took the initiative to cultivate and plant box. This proved successful and had far-reaching consequences, since box is still used for garden hedges.

Symmetrical gardens subdivided by hedges remained popular with the Mollets and Le Nôtre as well as with the seventeenth-century Dutchman Jan van der Groen, the author of *De Nederlandsche Hovenier*. Designers and architects such as Christiaan Huyghens, Jacob van Campen, Jacob Roman and Pieter Post laid out the Dutch symmetrical gardens copied by their contemporaries and subsequent generations.

The persecution of Protestants in seventeenth-century France caused many people to flee to other European countries where they hoped to find religious freedom. It was for that reason that the designer and architect Daniël Marot came to the Low Countries. His work on the houses, interiors and gardens of aristocratic families in the Netherlands and England brought him great fame. In his gardens, Marot used the same symmetrical style with hedges, parterres and walls.

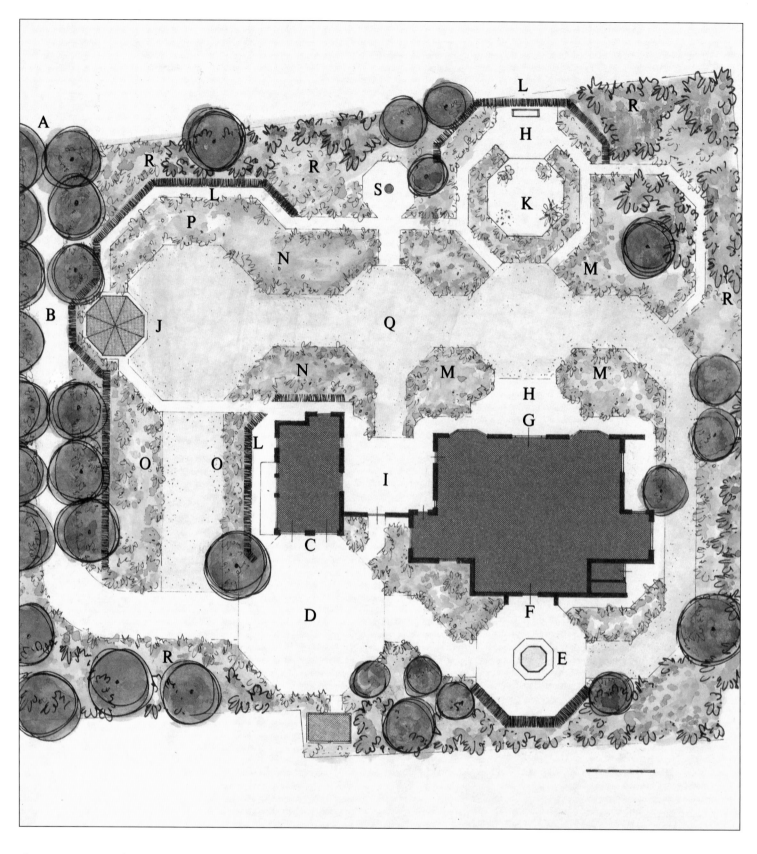

A	entrance to garden	N	white roses and purple perennials
B	wooded path, bamboo and Christmas roses	O	white and lemon yellow
C	garage	P	blue-flowered plants
D	parking area for cars	Q	grass
E	forecourt with ornament	R	tall old conifers and rhododendrons
F	front door	S	ornament
G	garden door		
H	terrace		
I	terrace with pots and dining table		
J	terrace with trellised arbour		
K	pond		
L	tall yew hedges		
M	pink roses, perennials with a lot of grey and blue		

In the wooded surroundings of Hilversum, handsome oaks and beeches form part of the background. Conifers have also been planted in the garden. Within such a tall and luxuriant framework, there may be a need for striking forms and surprise effects, and how better to achieve them than by means of hedges, yew hedges in this example. I based the entire layout on octagons and designed the pond and terrace to form an eye-catching focal point when seen from the house. A magnificent seat surrounded by pots was placed in front of the hedge.

The transverse axis consisted of a grass walk, with colourful borders starting with pink, blue and grey, followed by white and purple, then yellow and white, and finally blue. The blue borders are visible on entry to the garden, as is the roof of the trelliswork summerhouse, at the end of the central axis, where white was chosen in order to draw walkers towards it.

The planting beyond the hedges is almost colourless; the drive, for example, is bordered by bamboo, white hydrangeas, and green and white Christmas roses.

A terrace with large flower pots was constructed between the house and the garage, with an ecru-coloured Italian parasol to shade the dining table.

In the course of the eighteenth century, symmetry was condemned by a number of headstrong English designers, William Kent in particular, who began to design parks and gardens in a manner now known as the English landscape style. To them, symmetry was an abhorrence, at least in the parts of the garden that had to blend in with the surrounding countryside. Vegetable gardens, however, were allowed to keep their symmetrical forms.

Designers and owners of gardens became dissatisfied with these idealized landscaped gardens and men such as Humphrey Repton began to create more or less symmetrical rose and other flower gardens as well as orangeries close to the house, with the ever-popular landscaped areas of gardens and park beyond them. There were also men like Harold Peto, an English architect and a contemporary of Repton, who advocated a return to Italianate gardens with their symmetrical divisions. Peto designed a number of influential gardens, including Iford Manor Gardens, Buscot Park, Garinish Island and Ilnacullin in Ireland, for which the formula 'wild gardening after the manner of Robinson within the limits of Italian formality' was invented.

New ideas: asymmetry and symmetry

The architect Sir Edwin Lutyens took over many of Peto's ideas and reintroduced the symmetrical garden. Many other prominent designers, including Gertrude Jekyll, Lawrence Johnston and Vita Sackville-West, were working along similar lines.

All over Western Europe, designers were engaged in laying out gardens in this style. Some were entirely symmetrical, whilst others were designed as a blend of symmetrical and landscaped components. This type of design is known as the 'mixed style', *le style mixte*, or *mengstijl*.

Many contemporary landscape architects experienced to their cost how popular asymmetry remained in the years following the end of the Second World War. Hedges were tolerated, but not on both sides of a garden – that was regarded as stiff, old-fashioned and feudal. Asymmetry stood for an open mind, for socialism and for new challenges. Many owners of gardens believed – and still believe – that it was fashionable to create a hedge with a herbaceous border on one side of the garden, and an informal group of shrubs on the other. When the gardens of Walenburg Castle, created shortly after 1960, were opened to the public in the 1980s, many visitors discovered the beauty and excitement of the symmetrical layout chosen for most of the area. The symmetrical designs developed in the gardens at Sissinghurst, Hidcote and many other English houses earlier in the twentieth century, were revived once again at Walenburg Castle.

Symmetry was back, particularly in gardens divided by hedges into symmetrical sections. An ancient type of garden layout was revived, though no longer associated with stiffly clipped little trees and compartments filled with marble chippings. Instead, the various sections now contained romantic, scented roses, informally arranged, and herbaceous borders and shrubs forming sophisticated 'bouquets'. Hedges played an important role not only because of their beauty, but also because it was less expensive to grow them than to build walls. The number of wealthy owners of large gardens had dwindled over the years, and funds available for laying out gardens on a large scale were gradually reduced. The fact that fewer walls were built and many hedges were grown suggests, however, that people did not always allow for the amount of labour required for pruning and clipping them year after year.

The eye is cunningly drawn towards the distant parts of this garden. The wealth of plants behind the clipped yew shapes invites the stroller to go and discover the secrets beyond.
(Landscape architect André van Wassenhove, Bruges.)

Tall hedges for the subdivision of space

Anyone looking at gardens open to visitors will observe that hedges are not always an essential requirement for achieving a symmetrical layout. Many owners dislike the prospect of the ever-recurring task of clipping, while others still regard a clipped hedge as stiff or unnatural. There is every reason for seeking alternatives with rhododendron, holly or bamboo groves, any of which may serve as less formal, more or less maintenance-free dividers. An intriguing subdivision of space undoubtedly leads to an interesting garden.

Apart from the fact that building walls is usually too expensive, and often cannot be undertaken without town planning consent, there are several considerations in favour of subdividing gardens by planting hedges, in spite of their drawbacks.

Firstly, there is the deliberate contrast between the severely clipped dividers and the informal arrangement of trees, shrubs and flowering plants within them. Secondly, it is possible to vary the height of a clipped wall of plants oneself, something that is often far more difficult in the case of large shrubs or trees. To be able to maintain the ideal concept of the subdivision of space, it is necessary to know for certain that some dividers will have a fixed height. Thirdly, the hedge exists as a means of protection against the wind, unwelcome visitors, and the possibility of being overlooked. Enclosing one's own piece of land is, after all, the oldest reason for planting hedges.

There are naturally many other considerations that lead people to choose the effect of clipped 'walls' of shrubs or conifers illustrated in this book.

Which hedge goes where

An entire book could be devoted to the names of all the various plants that might be clipped into shape to form a hedge, or to the appropriate position for each type of hedge. It is possible, however, to provide a few basic rules. It would be unusual, for instance, to plant conifer hedges in an area of rivers, lakes and brooks. Privet or hawthorn would be more at home there. Beech and, in particular, hornbeam *(Carpinus betulus)* would also be appropriate.

In contrast, evergreen hedges of yew, holly or *Cupressocyparis* would be suitable for sandy areas where water is scarce, since they thrive naturally on dry soil where they can root deeply. The richer sandy soils are also suitable for beech *(Fagus sylvatica)* which can survive in conditions of severe drought, since it is also very deep rooted.

Privet grows anywhere and presents no problems as a hedge, at least in so far as growth is concerned. The roots, however, suck up all the nutrients from the surrounding soil, so that regular feeding is required if anything other than grass is to thrive in its vicinity. It is not hardy in conditions of extreme cold, and a hard frost may kill off its growth right down to the ground.

A laurel hedge, *Prunus laurocerasus* 'Rotundifolia', always appears to be something of an outsider. This kind of hedge is very popular among novice gardeners and, provided it is kept well clipped, it is certainly not ugly. With trees and shrubs behind it, and perennials or roses in front, it can even form quite a handsome hedge. However, it often creates a rather coarse and conspicuous effect because of its large leaves, which make it appear un-Dutch. Traditional gardeners therefore tend to despise laurel and opt for holly, yew, beech or hornbeam – and rightly so, since they are plants which go well with our native flora, woods and groves.

If there is a choice, try to select a hedge consisting of trees or shrubs native to the area where they are to grow. That would certainly help to achieve the kind of smooth transition between the garden and its surroundings to which one should really aspire.

Herbaceous Borders

Everyone dreaming of herbaceous borders thinks of England, where this garden phenomenon has developed into a true art form. The idea of two borders with a path between them is simple enough and can be copied by anyone. Yet it is not always possible to rely on achieving successful results if the interplay of proportion and colour has not been thought out properly.

I first saw one of the finest examples of a double border, the one at The Manor House, Bampton in Oxfordshire, illustrated in a British magazine, and subsequently in a great many books on gardens. It was designed by Countess Münster, who planned two combinations of pink and blue flowers with a grass walk in between them. The plants included *Centranthus*, roses, delphiniums, and a large number of other blue and white, pink and violet, and even brick-red flowering plants. Clumps of catmint, *Nepeta faassenii,* bordered the path.

It is unlikely that owners of gardens will actually copy borders like these. Most people are so keen on developing the individual character of their own garden that they will usually think up some layout and colour scheme themselves and rarely reproduce other designs indiscriminately. It is important, however, to take a good look at them and analyse what appears to be interesting and why that should be so.

There are several lessons to be learnt from Countess Münster's borders. Make sure that one type of plant, in this case *Nepeta*, is repeated all the way along the path. Also ensure that the width of the path bears a proper proportion to that of the borders. In this example, the width of each border is at least one and a half times that of the grass walk. Finally, make sure that there is a satisfactory build-up in the height of the plants. If the border is backed by a hedge, it is possible to achieve a sloping effect, with the tallest flowers up against the hedge or rising above it. Delphiniums, *Eupatorium* and tall phloxes are suitable. If there is no hedge at the back of the border, the tallest plants should be in the middle. With the lowest plants along the edges, the border will then assume an informal rounded form.

Abbots Ripton Hall

Gertrude Jekyll, known as 'the mother of the English border', wrote a great many books on colour schemes and plants with suitable colours for combining in herbaceous borders. She was not averse to quite colourful effects and boldly combined brownish orange and pink with yellow, white and blue, especially in long borders.

Mrs Merton's beautiful garden at The Old Rectory near Burghfield, Berkshire, includes these colourful, steeply rising borders where play is also made with shapes and sculpture. The majestic dark greens of deciduous trees and conifers are another important feature.

Photograph on pages 16/17: In this border at Walenburg Castle, Rosa 'Tuscany' has been trained upwards to provide a powerful vertical feature. The Dutch Garden Foundation (De Nederlandse Tuinenstichting) based in Amsterdam opens this garden to the public. Yews provide tranquillity as well as cheerfulness.

Jekyll's herbaceous borders, usually filled with perennials and occasionally a few roses, were often separated by a grass walk. When I visited what was left of her schemes, it struck me that, quite often, the borders were not backed by hedges.

Several impressive borders in Jekyll's style are to be found in the garden at Abbots Ripton Hall, Lord and Lady de Ramsey's Georgian house. A lawn at the back of the house borders on a small brook which flows from left to right and supplies fresh water. Beyond the brook, a broad path of mown grass extends between two borders and provides a fine vista from the house. The plants are brightly coloured, with the yellow and brownish orange shades of *Helenium* and *Hemerocallis* blending in with blues, whites and even pinks. These colours might be expected to clash, yet the overall effect is bright and cheerful.

Beyond the borders, the grass walk leads up to a handsome wrought-iron gate giving access to a further grass walk, this time uncut, between trees and shrubs.

This layout presents a number of instructive aspects. Firstly, it shows that, where there are long borders, it is necessary to use shades of yellow to hold people's attention. It also demonstrates that combining various shades of pink, blue, yellow, orange and purple in herbaceous borders is quite feasible. This may well come as a surprise to all single-colour-garden fanatics appalled at the very idea of combining pink and yellow. It is also worth noting that there are no hedges at the back of the Abbots Ripton borders. Instead, individual shrubs have been planted behind the perennials to add height where required, but they are regularly interrupted by glimpses of the grass beyond.

The borders are made up of large clumps of plants to avoid the confusion of colours and shapes that would have resulted otherwise. The existing bold patches of colour are easily distinguishable from a distance.

A focal point appears to be required at the end of a very long border. This may be a decorative gate, beyond which the grass path

Herbs are grouped informally in this long butterfly garden at the Garden Gallery in the Dutch province of Drenthe. The touches of yellow are provided by the Santolina *and chervil inside the edgings of clipped herbs.*

continues without borders, but there are many other ways of indicating the end of these colourful flower beds.

The architectural breaks in both herbaceous borders are yet another feature of Lord de Ramsey's garden. They consist of pyramidal wooden structures of great beauty which were designed by the architect in charge of the restoration of Westminster Abbey – hence their Gothic shape. They form memorable breaks in the flower beds bordering the central grass path and are a constant source of interest because of their unexpected shape and transparency.

Not everyone is likely to have such remarkable structures in their garden. It is more usual to find a large shrub, a round clipped yew, or a seat, vase or statue forming a break in a long border.

Laurence Johnston's red borders at Hidcote Manor

Red is not a colour that sensitive gardeners are likely to choose for their herbaceous borders, and I have rarely seen it used for such a purpose in the Netherlands, Belgium or France.

By combining red with the brown leaves of plants and shrubs such as red *Berberis*, red *Heuchera*, or brown-leafed, red-flowered dahlias, a genuine and renowned gardener managed to create two red borders in his garden, with a grass walk in between them. Red roses, red dahlias, cannas, perennials and foliage plants are grouped together in his garden at Hidcote Manor near Broadway along with decorative grasses to add grace and airiness.

This particular combination of plants was devised by Laurence Johnston, an American army officer who had lived for some years in France and England, and finally decided to create the large garden of his dreams in England, in the Cotswolds.

Simplicity of linear patterns at Jenkyn Place, Bentley, Hampshire. The mown pathway keeps this restrained exuberance of form and colour in check. Large borders need strong patches of colour to provide liveliness and rhythm where delicate shades would be too flat and insipid on their own. Red borders need dark perennials, annuals and shrubs such as the smoke tree (Cotinus coggygria 'Royal Purple') and berberis (Berberis ottawensis 'Superba'), which will have red berries among its purple leaves.

The planning of these borders may also be a source of inspiration. Annuals as well as bulbs and tuberous plants such as dahlias and cannas ensure that they are always full of flowers. Strong cluster-flowered roses help to provide blooms from summer until well into the autumn. The red leaves of the smoke tree (*Cotinus coggygria* 'Rubrifolia') and red hazel (*Corylus maxima* 'Purpurea') mingle with red-leafed *Berberis* in

Planting scheme for the pink border in Mr and Mrs Wintzen's garden at Driebergen in the Netherlands.

1   Hydrangea serrata *'Acuminata'*
2   Bergenia *'Morgenröte'*
3   Acanthus mollis
4   *ten round box trees*
5   Rosa *'Fragrant Delight'*
6   Fuchsia magellanica
7   Geranium versicolor
8   Acaena microphylla *'Kupferteppich'*
9   Polygonum amplexicaule
10 Anemone robustissima
11 Astilbe *'Europa'*
12 Saponaria ocymoides
13 Gypsophila *'Rosenschleier'*
14 Sedum telephium *'Herbstfreude'*
15 Rosa *'Ballerina'*
16 Astrantia major *'Rubra'*

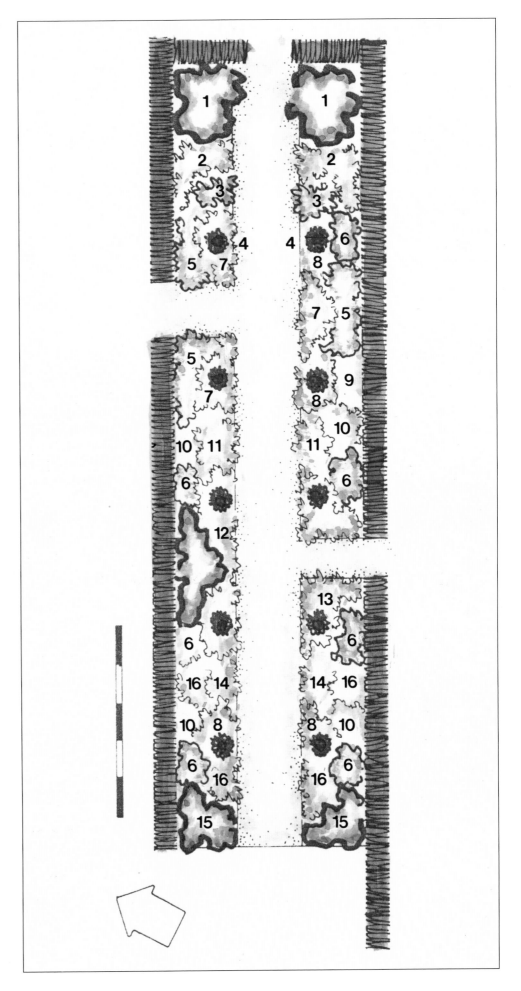

the background to give depth and support to the red flowers.

A graceful green shape, in this instance *Miscanthus sinensis* 'Gracillimus', provides a striking break in the red leaves and flowers, and catches the eye at times when there are too few flowers or even too great a profusion. Along with the shrubs and decorative grasses, the breaks in the hedges to prevent them from forming barriers have created a dancing display which is totally lacking in stiffness.

As a result of all these aspects, the garden comes as a complete surprise and offers the spectator all kinds of new ideas. Why should one not try to achieve a similar effect with blues, bronzes and near-blacks? There is no end to the search for harmony and variety, a game that is interpreted differently by every single gardener.

The double border at Walenburg Castle

It is not at all easy to maintain two more or less identical borders. That, at least, is what I learnt in the garden of Walenburg Castle. The garden was laid out in 1960 and a long space between two hedges was pro-vided with two borders of equal width separated by a grass path, about 32 in (80 cm) wide. A circle formed by curved yew hedges was created halfway along the borders, thus dividing them into two separate sections.

The section nearest the castle contains mainly white-flowered plants including white *Campanula persica*, white autumn anemones and white phloxes. The shrubs behind them include pink *Enkianthus campanulatus* and the striking but very lovely *Calycanthus floridus* with its wine-red flowers. The sole exception is *Paeonia ludlowii* which bears yellow flowers in spring.

Pink and white flowers occupy the further sections of the two borders. They include all the autumn-flowering plants such as pink autumn anemones, white *Cimicifuga racemosa* (bugbane) and two pink hydrangeas. There are all kinds of small bulbs and campions in spring, and in summer there are *Asperulas* and white shrub potentillas, so that there are always some flowers to admire, and usually a great many of them.

As Teus Mandersloot, the full-time gardener and I have been responsible for the selection of plants for many years, I take a keen interest in all the changes in the two borders. One of the problems is caused by the fact that one border faces south and is very sunny, whereas the other has shadows cast on it by the hedge at the back. Shade-loving plants grow taller on that side, but the sun-lovers languish. Problems such as these make it difficult to create genuinely symmetrical borders.

There are several instructive conclusions to be drawn from the Walenburg gardens. Genuine symmetry proves virtually impossible to achieve unless the borders run directly north–south. Since narrow borders do not provide room for enough plants, it is difficult to keep them permanently in flower and therefore sufficiently interesting. Because of

Left: The borders in the garden of The Priory, Kemerton, north-east of Tewkesbury in Gloucestershire, are some of the loveliest in England. In this one, red flowers are framed by shrubs with purple and bronze-coloured leaves.

André Eve's Jardin des Roses Anciennes at Pithiviers has achieved a seemingly accidental balance.
The meandering grass walk enables people to admire the roses from three different angles and avoids stiff linearity.

Several varieties of Astilbe *have been plan-*
ted in large groups on each side of the path
and thus create a balance in the garden of
Hodnet Hall, between Market Drayton and
Shrewsbury, Shropshire.

their early- or late-flowering habits, shrubs can add colour to a herbaceous border at times when perennials are not at their best. We planted bulbs such as *Camassia* in between the perennials to provide additional flowers too; this appears to have been successful. It also makes sense to add large-leafed plants to provide interest when there is nothing in flower.

Herb borders at the Garden Gallery

Traditionally, herbs are tucked away in between other plants or planted in convenient and easily accessible rectangular beds. They are rarely upgraded to become border plants. I first became aware of that possibility at Dartington Hall in Devon, where the famous American landscape architect Beatrix Farrand had designed a long herb border at the foot of a brick wall. All the way along the border there was a path edged on the other side by a row of twelve Irish yews (*Taxus baccata* 'Fastigiata') symbolizing the Twelve Apostles. Herbs are often associated with the Middle Ages since they were frequently ground, crushed or brewed for medicinal purposes. The symbolism of yews representing the Twelve Apostles is also medieval. This original combination of the two features avoided the stiffness of an historical interpretation and the long herb border had become an impressive feature.

Years later, when Frank van Linschoten and Pieter Baak asked me to design their large garden at Eext in the Dutch province of Drenthe, the memory of that long border at Dartington Hall kept crossing my mind. It is often possible to adapt an idea to fit in with a new situation. The outcome was two long herb borders backed by a couple of hornbeam hedges (*Carpinus betulus*). Between the borders there was a space which could be paved, grassed over or filled with a long channel of water. To avoid an untidy effect, it was decided to plant low-growing herbs in two long rectangular beds enclosed by paving. The low beds were edged with clipped herbs to differentiate them still further from the borders. This has created a special effect, and the surprise of it gives the garden its unusual character. Two junipers (*Juniperus communis*) were planted in the middle of the low beds, which adds perspective and rhythm to the somewhat uncontrolled growth of the herbs.

The borders contain fairly tall plants such as fennel, *Eupatorium* and the perennial grey-leafed, blue-flowered cardoon (*Cynara cardunculus*). Enclosed within its tall hornbeam hedge, the herb garden has become a pleasant courtyard to linger in and has therefore been provided with a permanent seat. This enables people to enjoy the scent of the various herbs while quietly watching the birds, bees and butterflies as they search for seeds, honey or nesting material.

Water in the Symmetrical Garden

There are four kinds of 'water' that can be used in gardens. Firstly, of course, there is natural water in the form of a river, a brook or a lake. Secondly, there is semi-natural water which is artificially introduced in a landscaped environment. Thirdly, there is the precisely enclosed type of water, again introduced artificially, which is likely to be contained in a round, square or rectangular pool. Finally, there is 'falling' water which, as a rule, has also been designed and artificially introduced by human ingenuity. Each of these four types of 'water' can be used to add a symmetrical feature to the layout of a garden.

Natural types of water

An unusual situation arose in the course of designing a garden near the small ancient town of Schuddebeurs in the Dutch province of Zeeland. The house had a lawn sloping down to a fairly large and almost round pool. This kind of natural pool, known locally as a *weel*, is in fact all that remains of water that flooded the land after a dyke had been breached. The dyke was subsequently repaired, leaving a pool of water on the landward side.

The plot was wider on one side than on the other, and at the design stage it was decided to divide it into a symmetrical part and one with a less formal layout. Such a scheme makes it possible to introduce a symmetrical element in an irregular plot by providing one part with a geometrical framework and giving the remainder a different function. By framing the symmetrical section with yew hedges and so introducing the effect of stage wings, the long sloping lawn suddenly became a series of separate spaces, while the view of the pond was naturally retained by way of contrast.

Newby Hall has one of the most interesting gardens in Yorkshire, and certainly one of the loveliest. The red-brick house was designed by famous architects and contains a magnificent art collection. The fascinating and surprising gardens were laid out by Major Edward Compton.

The basic structure of this garden is an example of a formal layout at its very best, with the land divided into separate sections which are gardens in themselves. Between the sections there are transitional areas which may be wooded, open, or designed in a totally different way. The double border with a central grassed walk is visible from the house and forms one of the finest parts of the large garden. The path ends at the foot of a grassy hill. A small river ripples gently along

Pieter Baak and Frank Linschoten wanted all kinds of aquatic creatures, birds and wild flowers at Eext, while I wanted a mirror in the shadow of an age-old oak tree. A bridge which is actually in the water almost enables one to walk on its surface.

Photograph on pages 26/27: The dark leaves of Prunus cerasifera 'Atropurpurea' make this pool still more mysterious, with all kinds of elongated leaf forms and plumes pointing like tentacles at the water-flies. (Nigel and Angela Azis' garden at Cook's Barn, West Burton, West Sussex.)

between the borders and the hill, separating the two worlds like a silver ribbon. The borders do not begin immediately outside the house. First there are steps, a terrace with some handsome ornaments such as vases and stone dogs, then a lawn and more steps before the long grass path descends towards the river. What makes this garden unique is the fact that the various sections have been allowed to slope down to the 'silver ribbon'. The herbaceous borders are quite colourful, but that should hardly come as a surprise. There is a golden rule which says that when perennials are used on a large scale, it is essential not to shrink from the use of contrasting colours to avoid a flat, insipid effect.

Semi-natural types of water

Low-lying types of rivers and brooks, meandering pools or round lakes such as occur in nature can also be created artificially. One of the advantages of 'imitating' natural types of water is that they can be located precisely where they look best in the overall design. The contrast between formality and informality remains the underlying principle. The actual design of the formal element depends on the owners of gardens and their consultants. It would be possible to create an entirely green garden with grass and hedges, or a flower garden full of

This raised pond was constructed in a formal but luxuriant private garden near Fontainebleau. All the components can be bought separately – a challenge to you to design an equally handsome variant of the above feature. The rose and the yellow flags give extra height to the fountain, which is quite modest in size.

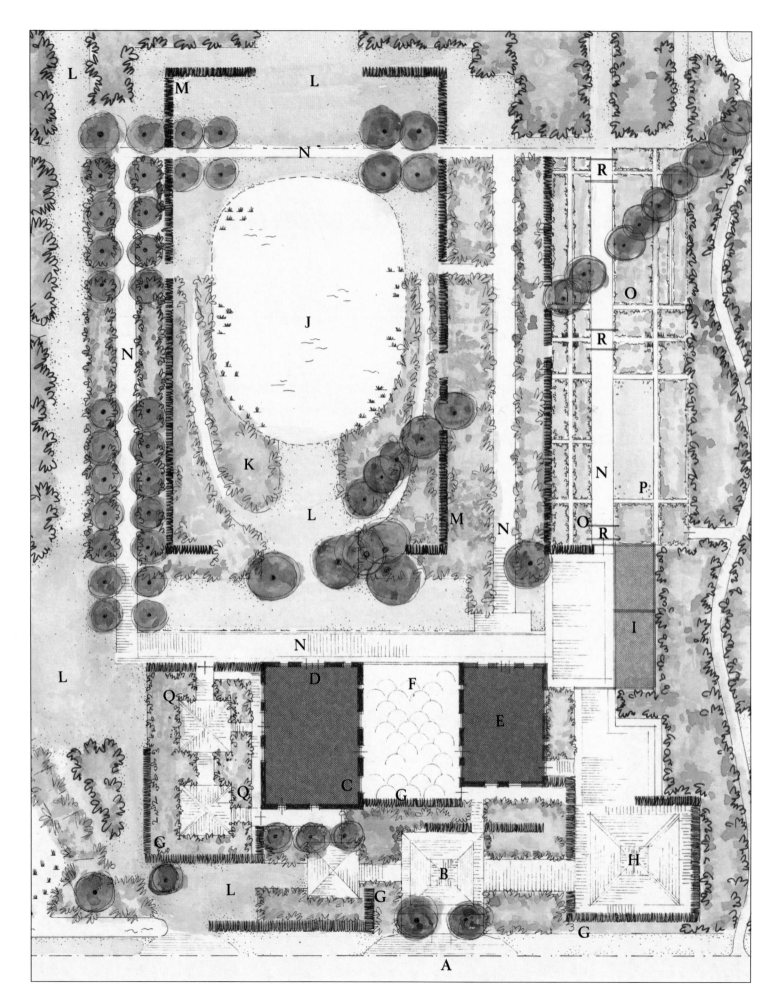

A Dutch farmhouse typical of the Lochem area with its almost identical barn needed an exciting garden – that, at least, is what my clients and I felt. They had moved there from the Reeuwijk lake district, and I thought a large pond would be appropriate – if only to prevent homesickness. It formed part of the view from the large windows in the living room and was surrounded by perennials allowing a further view through to the expected visiting deer. A strong beech hedge encloses this watery scene. Beyond the hedge there are paths lined with fruit trees (standard apples) and shrubs such as hydrangeas and ivy. A herb garden was laid out on the right, with areas to play games such as boules; to the left of the house there was a garden for yellow and orange cut flowers. In front, all was pink and shades of green, with a lot of beech hedges to provide form and act as space dividers.

A 26-foot (8-metre) long stone table was placed on the terrace between the farmhouse and the converted barn. The clinker bricks were laid out in a peacock-tail pattern and a wooden swing gate makes this an enclosed garden for the dog.

roses and/or perennials, with hedges marking the divisions. The basic principle, however, remains the quest for contrast in order to take advantage of both kinds of atmosphere without either of them disturbing the other.

Strictly geometrical types of 'water'

Water is one of the necessities of human life, a simple fact which has had enormous ramifications. Stimulated by the desire to have everything that is useful near to them, people have always devised all kinds of solutions to the problem of introducing and designing the shape of water in their immediate vicinity.

One of the oldest examples is undoubtedly to be found in the colourful picture of a garden that a high official in ancient Egypt had painted on a wall of his tomb. The garden was situated on one of the banks of the Nile and irrigated with river water to make it suitable for the cultivation of grapes, vegetables and fruit trees. Flowers for cutting are often recognizable too in similar illustrations. There were also ponds in geometrical shapes, usually rectangular. The entire water system in this garden – ponds and canals – was interlinked. This pattern of artificially introduced and formally designed water clearly indicates the connection between the shape of the water feature and the rest of the formally designed utilitarian garden.

This principle persisted for centuries: the garden and any form of water in it or alongside it were designed as a single unit, in a single style. Water in severe geometrical shapes thus became an architectonic form in the gardens of Greeks, Romans, Turks and Arabs in Asia Minor, North Africa, Spain and Portugal, and, because of its specific nature, could be used as a mirror, to bring good fortune, as a place for fish or water plants, or as a swimming pool. The actual shapes changed over the years from long narrow rectangles to octagons, circles or even squares.

'Falling water'

In mountainous regions one can see how water cascades down in waterfalls, gurgles through fissures in rocks or ripples over stones. Mankind has always been fascinated by the beauty of falling water, and the way in which this natural phenomenon has been introduced in gardens is worthy of our admiration. In southern countries, the art of so conducting water that it could fall from a fountain into a basin without modern equipment such as pumps was mastered centuries ago. Using natural differences in land levels, people managed to bring water supplies from higher areas to villages and cities by way of ingenious systems of conduits and pipes. Inside the houses, the water could then be forced up under pressure to the levels required for spouts and fountains. The technology developed by the Romans was

often applied for fountains and ponds. Even in the Netherlands, this technology was formerly used in a few places to which natural water could be conducted from a higher level. Nowadays, of course, electrically powered pumps make it possible to pipe water from a reservoir to a fountainhead wherever it may be required. Choosing a suitable design for the reservoir and fountainhead is all that remains to be done, but it is of vital importance for the creation of the appropriate atmosphere.

Antique and pseudo-antique fountain ornaments

Heads of gods or animals have been used for centuries as a source of inspiration for more or less successful fountain ornaments. Genuine antique fountainheads made of marble, bronze, stone or occasionally terracotta soon became priceless ornaments. They were frequently decorated with fish heads. Dolphins, in particular, became a prominent feature of fountain ornaments.

It is fortunate that there are skilled craftsmen, especially in Italy, who continue to copy antique models. Copies such as these may be important if a fountain or waterspout needs to be installed in an historical setting. Rather than choosing anything modern, people often prefer to place an ornament inspired by antiquity near an old house or an official building.

This kind of fountain ornament in traditional style can also be quite functional – and certainly very beautiful – indoors, in a hall, a conservatory, a bathroom or even a lavatory. It may well be, however, that house and garden owners are often hesitant to use such objects light-heartedly, and would shudder at the thought of allowing the jet of a fountain or even a shower to emerge from the jaws of a marble or bronze lion. Perhaps this attitude will change when they realize that ornaments are there for us to enjoy and not just to look at in museums!

Modern fountain ornaments

A modern fountain can be created by having a semicircular recess hollowed out of the top of a square block of blue stone. The block of stone is then built into the wall so as to project from it. A water supply pipe is fixed to the back of the wall, and a hole leading to the pipe is drilled through the wall immediately above the centre of the stone ornament.

As soon as water is pumped upwards, it can pass through the opening into the stone fountainhead and splash into a pond or basin below. In Italy, semicircular bowls, frequently made of roughly hewn marble, are often fitted above ground level to catch the water. These handsome ornaments with shallow semicircles sometimes provide little space for the pump needed to force the water up to the higher level again. With a little ingenuity, however, it is usually possible to find a space where a pump can be fitted behind a wall. The mechanism required for a fountain by a pond is easier to install as there is always room for a pump at ground level.

Ponds

Few garden features appeal more to the imagination than ponds. Their design has not changed much over the centuries, which proves to what extent rectangular, square and round forms are to be found almost as a matter of course in environments created by human beings.

The large oblong pool in the gardens of Emperor Hadrian's villa at Tivoli near Rome is undoubtedly one of the world's most beautiful examples and has been restored to its former glory. One end of the pool is rounded and, at the junctions with the long sides, a plinth holding a statue projects into the water to create a narrowing effect which has been much imitated.

There are statues and columns supporting arches on the low wall enclosing the pool. The whole complex gives a good idea of the appearance of a pool in a large garden in the heyday of the Roman empire: richly decorated and beautifully shaped. Hadrian's garden pool has a classical shape which is still very popular all over the world for ponds as well as for indoor and outdoor swimming pools.

Rectangular ponds

The rectangle is undoubtedly one of the most popular shapes for a pond. A long, straight and narrow feature gives the kind of taut linear effect that goes well with either modern or more traditional architecture. It may be bordered by grass, or by perennials, roses or herbs, but the pond's simple shape will guarantee tranquillity and a powerful interplay of lines. Seating is often provided at one end, from where one can look across at a vista on the opposite side. It is advisable to let

some plants luxuriate there as well, so that the outline of the pond becomes slightly blurred.

A first impressive introduction to long rectangular ponds awaits many visitors to the French gardens designed by André le Nôtre, especially the grandiose examples at Versailles. The final stretch of water which, when seen from the palace, extends furthest into the countryside, is a long straight pond rightly called the Grand Canal. In days gone by, people in pleasure craft could enjoy cruising on it, but the effect of the reflecting water as a sublime transition to the flat grassland beyond is more important. Water and meadows appear to merge into each other and there seems to be no end to the canal. The long rows of Italian poplars beyond the canal reinforce the perspective view and are equally memorable.

An encounter with long ponds from a still earlier period awaits anyone visiting two remarkable gardens at Granada. One of them is world famous: the Generalife, the summer residence of the Moorish rulers in the Alhambra, contains a very long and narrow canal which gives perspective and radiance to a walled flower garden. The second pond is less well known and is to be found at El Chapiz, in the garden of the Arabic Language Institute not far from the Alhambra. At the back of a secluded house, an unexpected patio, open on one side, contains a long narrow pond surrounded by potted orange trees. Tall old cypresses are lined up at the end of the pond, thus obscuring the patio from view. There are white walls, windows, doors, and an old wooden veranda on the first floor. Beyond the house there is an equally fascinating garden which is symmetrically subdivided by box and cypress hedges. The air is scented with the perfume of many roses, the atmosphere is enchanting and its memory is something to cherish for ever.

My gardening friend Jolande Van de Maele is always making changes in her garden. This is her latest addition: a contemporary water garden with nearly all the flowers in shades of blue and mauve. Agapanthus *is grown in pots, while the iron Cupid lovingly allows the water to circulate.*

Right: *Beside the pond, low-growing lady's mantle* (Alchemilla mollis) *covers the edge with delicate yellow flowers, while* Polygonum bistorta *on this side of the seat lets its pinkish white spikes dance in the wind.*
The garden of Monsieur and Madame Sainte-Beuve, Planbessin in Normandy.

Square and rectangular

An inspiring combination of these two shapes is to be found at the starred restaurant Het Laurierblad at Berlare in Belgium. A square pond is situated more or less in the centre of the attractive inner garden. The square, edged with blue stone, is raised about 12 in (30 cm) above the level of the land.

Four stone water-spouts are fitted at the sides, with water from them splashing continuously into the pond. The edge is just slightly lower on one side, thus creating a waterfall. The water cascades into a long straight pond extending in the direction of the restaurant. All this provides a fascinating spectacle from the restaurant's sun lounge, and visitors can also sit out of doors on the terraces and enjoy the sounds of splashing water intermingling with the bird song.

Round ponds

Any designer working with pen and paper often views the world as seen from above. This is certainly true of architects and landscape architects. It often looks good to create a circle at the place where two roads or paths cross; the circle may be a plaza or, when it is in a park or a garden, some kind of pond. Perhaps the round pond came into being in that way – as an enlarged junction. Round ponds are infinite, self-enclosed worlds. By adding stone on one side and plants on the other, it is possible to break through the symmetry of the curves or, if the hardened sections and planting are also arranged symmetrically, to increase the balance instead. One needs to play around with circular ponds, or else just accept them as quiet reflecting surfaces.

A round pond of great beauty may be admired at Knightshayes Court. This large garden near Tiverton in Devon has everything one might expect: a view of hills and meadows, old trees, a rhododendron garden, a wooded garden and a few handsome formal enclosed gardens. One of them is particularly beautiful. It lies within an old yew hedge clipped in the form of crenellations and enclosing a grass-filled patio. The round pond is situated in the centre of this green patio. Near it, there is a small grey-leafed ornamental pear tree (*Pyrus salicifolia*), and a beautiful female statue is situated in the patio's central north-south access. This figure and the grey tree with its gracefully suspended twigs add further interest to the otherwise tranquil garden. One can sit on a stone seat and reflect how simple a beautiful garden can be.

Left: *People emerging from a broad pergola supporting ancient apple trees encounter these four box 'custodians' surrounding water lilies. The pebbles are also rounded, a small detail elevated to an art form with the same enthusiasm as is found in the larger components of this richly varied garden. (Heale House, Upper Woodford, near Salisbury, Wiltshire.)*

Arches and Pergolas

An arch for supporting roses, clematis, fruit trees or wistarias is an old-fashioned garden feature which has now been revived. It is always difficult to tell when and where a desire for such romanticism first arises, making it virtually impossible to point to any one designer as being the original source of inspiration. Besides, many old gardens have always been embellished with arches and pergolas and numerous people have been inspired by their examples.

Roseraie de l'Haÿ

I have rarely seen so many arches in a single area as in this rose garden, which was designed by the famous French landscape architect Edouard André. There are pergolas covered in roses and single iron arches intended exclusively for roses. There is also a summer-house constructed entirely of trellis, and this structure too is overgrown with roses.

The Roseraie de l'Haÿ is a garden devoted to the queen of flowers, the rose. It was not intended to be a mere rose garden, but was required to be a museum of the rose as well. All kinds of ancient roses have therefore been brought together in its various sections.

There is, for example, a section with biblical roses or, at least, those which are to be found in countries mentioned in the Bible. All the wild roses growing in the countries of Asia Minor, Italy and France have been planted in this section.

There is also the collection of Joséphine de Beauharnais, Empress of France, who led such a sad life after Napoleon had divorced her. The artist Redout recorded many of her roses, and at the Roseraie they can be seen in reality.

A third section is devoted to nineteenth-century roses, and includes a huge collection of old-fashioned but still usable climbers with beautiful blossoms and scent. They are trained over the numerous arches and taken down every year so that the old branches can be removed. The new shoots that will flower profusely the following year are then tied back into position. Each arch consists of two separate iron arches linked by strong wire netting and painted dark green. The climbing rose therefore has a wide frame to which the branches can be tied, and the twine is easy to insert through the netting. It is a delight to find that all the climbing cluster-flowered double roses, so popular with our grandparents and now threatened with obsolescence, still thrive in this unique rose garden.

Photograph on pages 40/41: *The live museum of the rose is situated south of Paris at l'Haÿ-les-Roses. Biblical roses, wild roses from many different countries, and the Joséphine de Beauharnais Collection are interspersed with old climbing roses, all identified on name tags. They are supported by round arches or rectangular structures and are untied annually for pruning.*

In this garden at Fontainebleau, a youthful kiwi is trained over an iron arch, copying those covered in roses. The slightly raised flower pot set up in what I should call 'stylish simplicity' is also rounded.

'Madame' was responsible for yet another section. She was the wife of the prime mover in the establishment of this garden, the director of Le Bon Marché chain of department stores. She was given her own section in this labour-intensive garden, which cost so much money to lay out and maintain. This part was therefore named 'Madame'. It contains modern roses with long flowering seasons, something that the old varieties lack. Many colours and flowering habits, from large- to cluster-flowered and climbing roses, have been brought together here. Madame could therefore always cut some flowers for her boudoir. Nowadays, of course, the roses are no longer cut, but remain on the plants for the benefit of visitors who, after the main flowering period of the old roses in late June and July, can continue to see a great deal of colour and many flowers.

The Roseraie de l'Haÿ is situated in the Paris suburb of l'Haÿ-les-Roses, formerly a pleasant village on the outskirts of the great metropolis. The village centre with its ancient church and large number of small shops has retained its rural character. You can buy delicious wine and rolls there, and enjoy them with cheese or charcuterie in the park adjoining the rose garden.

It is interesting to take another look at the designer of this garden, Edouard André. This highly successful landscape architect and author of respected books, designed one of the most beautiful pergolas in the Netherlands. His name will always be associated with that country because of the garden of Weldam Castle which he designed for the aristocratic Bentinck-Solms family.

The pergola at Weldam Castle

When Edouard André came to the Netherlands to design a large castle garden, he had the advantage that Hugo Poortman, an assistant who worked in his Paris office, was familiar with conditions in the Netherlands. Hugo Poortman had been apprenticed to the French grandmaster for a number of years, this being the only way of qualifying as a landscape architect at a time when there were no specialized training courses for the purpose. Poortman was to remain involved during the entire execution of André's grandiose scheme and, in his subsequent position as the estate's steward, became responsible for the impeccable maintenance of the master plan.

If we look at the scheme for the castle garden, we appear to be admiring a seventeenth-century layout. Nothing, however, could be further from the truth. Although the elements of the design – the parterre of box garlands, the long hornbeam (*Carpinus betulus*) pergola and the maze – are all seventeenth-century garden features, this was a design conceived in the nineteenth century. The historical components are expertly grouped near the old castle. André had a deep knowledge of garden history. He chose to lay out a formal seventeenth-century garden near the castle and create a landscaped park around it, leaving the existing elements intact.

A pergola consists of many iron arches

Anyone wishing to create a pergola should first consider how to achieve the rounded form required for shrubs or conifers. The mere pruning of branches sometimes makes it possible first to let the shrubs grow up as a straight wall and then to make the upper parts assume a rounded form. The backs and tops are subsequently pruned and a natural arch is thus achieved.

Usually, however, people would rather be sure than sorry, and therefore construct a framework over which the branches of shrubs or conifers can be trained. Iron arches are often used for the purpose, but in old gardens wood was also used to make the required forms. A splendid example is to be seen at the Palace of Het Loo in the Netherlands. There, in Mary Stuart's Queen's Garden, is a wooden construction with hornbeam trained over it.

Iron arches were chosen at Weldam. Following André's scheme, Hugo Poortman planted hornbeam (*Carpinus betulus*) up against them. The trees have actually grown so tall and strong that the heavy iron construction has been lifted right out of the ground in several places. The arches are now as it were suspended in the branches that have grown right round them.

Weldam's pergola is not unique in world terms but the reason why it is so special is that openings in its east wall give access to it from the box parterre. These apertures allow light to penetrate the otherwise dark tunnel of greenery. Especially in the mornings, the light of the rising sun falls in broad bands across the dark pergola, thus creating a fascinating interplay of light and shade. At the end of the tunnel, a window has been left open to allow a glimpse of the trees and the maze beyond.

Monsieur and Madame Sainte-Beuve have created a vista in their garden at Planbessin in Normandy. There are not any rows of clipped trees here. Instead, there is the austere modern rhythm of wooden posts and wistaria. The colours are bluish grey, soft gold and green, which seem to create space.

A pergola of pear trees

Anyone setting out to create a pergola need not choose between the rather sombre hornbeam and yew. There are other options for covering this kind of green tunnel. Pear trees have long been used for the purpose and create a most attractive, if somewhat time-consuming,

Plants growing over Arches 1–7:

1 Wistaria sinensis
2 Vitis 'Rembrandt'
3 Rosa filipes *and* Clematis alpina
4 Vitis 'Purpurea'
5 Wistaria sinensis 'Alba'
6 Akebia quinata
7 Rosa 'Climbing Schneewittchen' and
   Clematis alpina
8 Rhododendron 'Cunningham's White'
9 Cornus alba 'Elegantissima'
10 Miscanthus sinensis 'Gracillimus'
11 Viburnum davidii
12 Aconitum henryi 'Spark'
13 Viburnum plicatum
14 Aster amellus 'Joseph Lakin'
15 Campanula lactiflora 'Loddon Anna'
16 Aster alpinus
17 Delphinium 'Völkerfrieden'
18 Calamintha nepeta
19 Sinarundinaria murielae
20 Pulmonaria angustifolia 'Azurea'
21 Buddleia davidii 'Ile de France'
22 Phlox divaricata 'Dirgo Ice'
23 Gypsophila 'Rosenschleier'
24 Stachys byzantina 'Cotton Ball'
25 Nepeta sibirica
26 Lysimachia ephemerum
27 Agastache foeniculum
28 Hydrangea serrata 'Blue Bird'
29 Prunus lusitanica
30 Lithodora diffusa
31 Hosta sieboldiana 'Elegans'
32 Hibiscus – blue
33 Campanula lactiflora 'Prichard's Variety'
34 Rosa 'Lady of the Dawn'
35 Macleaya cordata
36 Veronica longifolia 'Blauriesin'
37 Campanula poscharskyana 'Lisduggan'
38 Decaisnea fargesii
39 Molinia altissima
40 Phlox paniculata-hybr. 'Lavendelwolke'
41 Aronia arbutifolia 'Brilliant'
42 Salvia nemorosa 'Ostfriesland'
43 Lavandula
44 Anemone hybrida 'Honorine Jobert'
45 yew hedges

The walkway leading up to this ivy-covered house is flanked by tall yew hedges. Gaps in the hedges provide glimpses of the garden to the left and right. The blue garden comes into view on the right. A long grass walk emphasizes the length of the space, while arches covered in roses, clematis and black grapes provide visual breaks. Paths and terraces are made of simple rectangular paviors made of grey concrete.

Planting scheme for the blue border in Mr and Mrs De Gruyter's garden.

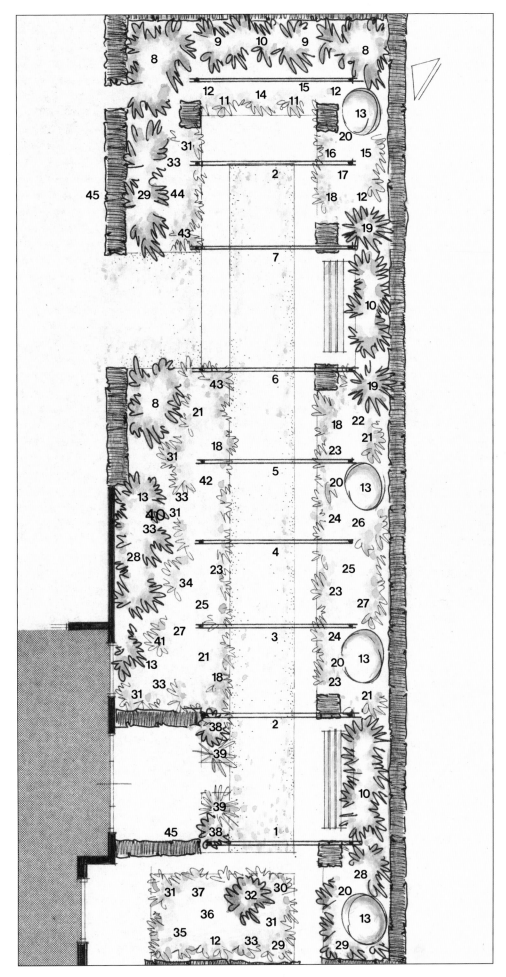

The rose garden at Mottisfont Abbey near
Romsey contains rustic oak frames which are
as simple as they are successful. They are
grey, with grey lichen growing over them.
Rosa 'Tuscany' here displays its velvety
deep-violet blooms, with white foxgloves
standing out among the roses.

version of this feature. Their white flowers appear in spring and, if properly pruned, the trees will bear abundant fruit. The required work is carried out in both summer and winter. Winter pruning consists of removing all suckers and dense branches; suckers are removed again in summer to preserve all the tree's strength for fructification. Occasionally it may also be necessary to tie in a branch which has grown or sagged beyond the outline of the pergola.

As most of the work needs to be done during the winter, a pear-tree pergola is not an unwise choice since there are fewer tasks such as mowing, trimming roses or tying up perennials to perform during that season.

It is advisable to use iron arches, which need to be joined together with long strips in several places. Anyone wishing to see this kind of construction should go and look at the castle gardens at Arcen, in the Dutch province of Limburg, where a perfect combination of arches and long continuous tubing has been created. This pergola has hornbeam rather than fruit growing over it. Instead of the ever-popular dark green, a handsome shade of dark blue has been used to paint the tubular framework; it goes surprisingly well with the green of the hornbeam.

Arches with climbing plants: Claar de Gruyter's blue garden

The French and Italian gardens of the renaissance and baroque periods have made us realize that long spaces can have a dramatic effect. It is important, however, for the sides of the space to be walled or hedged more or less uninterruptedly; otherwise it is a field rather than a space.

The large garden surrounding a modern bungalow at Vught in the Dutch province of North Brabant contains just such a long strip. It was decided to create a grass walk between two borders planted with perennials and shrubs with bluish-grey leaves. The shrubs include all kinds of buddleias and *Ceanothus*; blue-flowered perennials such as *Iris sibirica*, *Geranium* 'Johnson's Variety', and many varieties of *Veronica* were collected and planted along with blue-leafed *Hosta*.

The effect was just as desired: dramatic and striking. Even so, my clients Claartje and Josef de Gruyter felt there was something missing in their long garden. It was decided to construct wide arches over the grass walk, each one consisting of a single tube. They were anchored to the ground with strong concrete posts; this is essential if vigorous climbers are to be grown up the arches. That is what happened here:

wistarias, blue-flowered *Campanula* and *Vitis* 'Rembrandt', which produces black grapes, were planted against the arches, along with white

roses to add cheerful and exuberant flowers to the rhythm of rounded forms. The effect is not only attractive at eye level, but the lines of shadow cast on the green grass are major plus-points and create a rhythm which suggests depth.

A long space always has two viewing-points: at the beginning and at the end. In this garden, a Lutyens seat was placed at the end, and a witch ball surrounded by a number of beautiful plants at the beginning.

A graceful *Buddleia alternifolia* overhangs the silver-coloured glass ball which is placed on a pedestal. The *Buddleia* has beautiful small bluish-purple flowers crowded on to graceful twigs. A box peacock is another plant featured here. *Brunnera, Hosta* and *Viola* are included for their effect in summer.

Rose arches in Claude Monet's garden

A great many arches were used in gardens in the late-nineteenth century, particularly in kitchen gardens or at the entrance to separate gardens with roses, herbs, vegetables or flowers for cutting.

One of the best-known gardens with arches – entirely restored not so long ago – once belonged to the French Impressionist painter Monet. When his heirs no longer had enough money to maintain the property, it was decided to open the house and garden at Giverney in Normandy to visitors, along with the artist's studio.

Visitors flocked there in unexpectedly large numbers. They can now look at the beautiful pond with the water-lilies that Monet painted so sublimely, and also admire the rows of peonies, irises, tulips and dahlias planted in large numbers near the house. Wide iron arches made of metal sections and painted an unusual shade of green have been erected over the entrance path which once led directly from the road to Monet's front door. This colour was also used for painting the wooden parts of the house.

After much thought, I came up with what seemed to me an acceptable theory about the choice of this bluish shade of green, so

Claartje de Gruyter's Pink Garden at Vught, a straight path leads up to two staggered yew hedges, with the path continuing in between them. On the left there is tall Eupatorium purpureum; Geranium endressii *drifts happily across the path, and* Rosa 'Betty Prior' *combines with* Phlox paniculata 'Aida' *to provide touches of bright violet, and yet ... something was lacking. I then set up dark-green iron arches with apples and quinces growing over them, and my design acquired balance.*

Left: *What might appear rather too austere in a drawing, can be softened as if by magic with some delicate touches. The arches are almost square and are repeated to provide harmony.*
(Lower Hall, Worfield, Shropshire. Source: Gardens of England and Wales, 1994 ed.)

typical of the Dutch country round Zaandam, which contrasts so well with the greens in nature. Monet made a lengthy visit to the Netherlands to paint the bulb fields. He was immensely fascinated by colours and their effect, which explains his interest in the brightly coloured fields with their separate sections for the various contrasting shades of tulips, hyacinths, narcissi and grape hyacinths, all in contrasting colours.

In the course of his visit, Monet also wandered through the province of North Holland, where he discovered the River Zaan. He found, just north of Amsterdam, a world of wooden houses painted bright or dark green, now known as the Zaandam houses. There were many sawmills along the Zaan, where wood was sawn into planks and the poor population had decided centuries ago to use wood for building their houses rather than the expensive bricks employed elsewhere in the Netherlands. Each village had its own colour for painting the houses. It was bright green at Koog aan de Zaan, grey in the small village of Broek in Waterland, and dark green at Twiske. Monet very much liked the bright shade of green that he saw there and recorded the houses in several of his paintings.

Pink and yellow roses have been trained over the arches. *Rosa* 'Golden Shower' and *Rosa* 'New Dawn' flower profusely over a long period, so that that there is always colour to be seen on the bright green iron constructions. The combination of pink and yellow is unusual but interesting. Bright red, which would have added an ordinary and vulgar touch, has fortunately been avoided. Very wide borders full of flowering plants have been created under the arches and contain shrub, floribunda and cluster-flowered roses. Numerous bulbs have also been planted here and also, for instance, *Eremurus*, which bears yellow, white or pink flowers. Peonies, lilies and many other flowers may be found in this garden.

After the eleventh of May, groups of *Nasturtium* are planted out along the broad entrance path and allowed to grow over it during the summer. They drift across the light-coloured path, thus creating a further sense of depth. There are old yew trees near the house, yet there is enough light for large flower beds filled with exuberant pink- and red-flowered plants. As a result of all this, the garden once again provides the fascinating interplay of form and colour recognizable in Monet's paintings by all who enjoy studying his work.

Flowering plants grown in large greenhouses and local nurseries are always kept in readiness for planting out in the garden – there must be colour! This custom, started by Monet, has also been reintroduced.

Ornaments

Anyone studying the ancient architecture of the Egyptians, Greeks, Romans and later Western civilizations will discover how important a part was played by symmetrical design. Clearly, there was a need for balance in a world that was so unpredictable, so mysterious. Although symmetry in its most extreme form does not occur in nature, people wanted their architecture to emphasize the fact that they could confront the natural world with their own power. The Egyptian temples are symmetrical, as are those of the Greeks and Romans. Even gardens were laid out in symmetrical patterns so as to demonstrate yet again that man was in control.

The oriental way of thinking was very different, and in China and Japan gardens were deliberately asymmetrical to demonstrate their harmony with nature. Far-eastern nations may have idealized nature as an ideal of beauty for thousands of years, but that did not occur in Western culture.

The desire to express power and vigour by means of symmetry in buildings and gardens continued for centuries, and it was not until the development of Art Nouveau, Art Deco and the Bauhaus style that architects ventured to design asymmetrical buildings. Designers of parks and gardens, however, had abandoned symmetrical layouts at an earlier date, particularly as a result of the English landscape style with its lack of uniformity.

Ornaments are closely linked to buildings and gardens, which explains why they were often placed symmetrically in the past. Symmetrical arrangements of pots, seats and statues are currently in vogue once again, thus demonstrating the persistent influence of these fundamental concepts.

Statuary

It is interesting to observe that modern sculptures are unlikely to be placed symmetrically in a garden. Their creators – famous sculptors such as Henry Moore, Maillol, Zadkine, Charlotte van Pallandt, Frank Stella, to name but a few – would be appalled to think that their idiosyncratic creations should be arranged in that way. It is therefore essential to look for other ornaments which are suitable for displaying symmetrically in the garden.

In my opinion, statues copied from older models, or original antiquities of a former age, are especially appropriate for symmetrical

Photograph on pages 52/53: *Those who dare may win or lose. Orange wallflowers look cheerful here in the spring garden. The Neo-Gothic seats in the garden of Hazelbury Manor in Wiltshire, unsurpassed in the beauty and power of its architecture, look equally inviting. Anyone combining strength and cheerfulness may lose or, so it seems to me, win!*

The architect Elias Canneman designed this greenhouse for Walenburg, a small Dutch castle; his wife Liesbeth added the wealth of herbs. The crazy paving is made of blue stone from Namen in Belgium.
(Walenburg te Langbroek in the Dutch province of Utrecht.)

arrangements. Two nymphs or fauns or satyrs look very good standing on their plinths in an area of the garden divided into equal parts. Modern sculptures, however, are rarely arranged symmetrically.

There are innumerable new copies of old statues available, often beautifully cast, like those produced by two English firms, Haddonstone and Chilstone. They copy English statues and their plinths, thus enabling people to have perfect sand-coloured reproduc-

tions in their gardens. Their rich collections include Cupids and other figures of children. The boy warriors, naked children wearing helmets and carrying bows and arrows, are my favourite Chilstone figures. Roy Strong, the distinguished museum director and author of books on gardens, has some in his garden, and I have had them in mine for years.

Obviously, there are other ornaments which are more generally suitable and may well be included in a symmetrical arrangement.

Garden vases of Classical design

Many old gardens contain vases, often pot-shaped forms with lids. If there is no lid, it is more usual to call them pots, as they can have plants or even small shrubs growing in them.

Lidded garden vases are often to be found in the countries of northern Europe, where winters are severe and frost could make the earth in pots expand and cause cracks. A lid placed on top of the pot ensures that the soil inside is less likely to freeze.

What began as a practical solution, developed into a separate art form over the centuries, so that decorative lidded vases are common throughout the world. Vases are sometimes placed on plinths to make them more visible and to raise them above hedges, roses and shrubs.

Open garden vases were first used in countries such as Greece and Italy. Especially in the latter, beautiful marble vases, often decorated with interesting sculpture, are still to be found in many gardens. The numerous gods of the Greek and Roman world were venerated with offerings of flowers. Temple vases were filled with flowers or

Laurus nobilis is the botanical name for the bay tree, the leaves of which can be used for culinary purposes. The garlanded pots filled with herbs by the owners of the Garden Gallery are references to the Mediterranean aspects of their garden at Eext in the Dutch province of Drenthe.

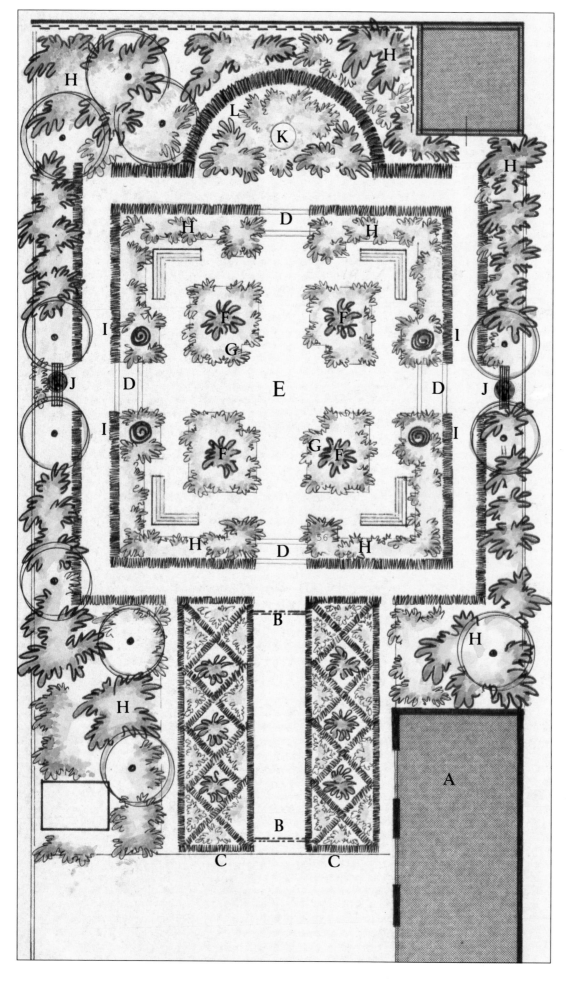

A end of long walk, also entrance to garden
B wooden ivy-covered arches
C box parterre with standard roses, white and pinkish-blue perennials
D stone steps
E a sunken area (18 in/45 cm deep) for sitting, watching and walking
F pointed yews
G clipped box
H mixed hedges with hydrangeas, holly, Escallonia *and so on*
I low box hedge
J two dark green cast-iron vases on plinths
K sandstone goddess in a central position
L tall box hedge

I designed this formal garden at the rear of a bank facing the Herengracht in Amsterdam. The centre area consists of a sunken garden with eight dark-green seats where people can enjoy a picnic. A less than life-sized antique statue is placed as a focal point along the central visual axis as seen from inside the house. This makes the garden look longer than it is in reality. I designed the box-edged beds to introduce some perspective; all the lines are directed towards the back of the garden. The freely grouped shrubs provide romanticism; formal and evergreen aspects are provided by the clipped-box compartments with yew cones. A handsome terrace paved with warm clinker bricks adjoins the building.

vines, and embellished with garlands of fruit. It was partly due to the tradition of placing vases permanently outside public buildings that the idea of arranging similar models in gardens arose.

Vases were either carved out of marble or modelled in terracotta. Terracotta perishes, however, whereas marble is more durable, another reason why it is still possible to admire antique marble vases in museums and historical gardens. The reliefs carved on vases often represented mythological scenes or events and people of importance in the days of their creators.

In no other country is there a greater sense of the need to preserve the beauty of the past than in Italy. It is therefore hardly surprising that historical garden vases, or at least some of them, are copied in that country. Models universally admired centuries ago are on sale there in marble, terracotta and sometimes even in bronze.

Lead garden vases

In addition to clay and bronze, lead is also used frequently for garden vases in order to increase sales of handsome models or to produce a number of copies of a particular design for one and the same garden. A mould is made first, and the liquid metal is then poured into it. Many antique types of garden ornament are still reproduced in lead. This is fortunate, since it preserves the model and enables enthusiasts to buy copies at reasonable prices.

One of the principal lead casters was Van Nost (Van Oost), a Dutch sculptor who was highly successful in producing castings in the days of William and Mary. Van Nost also designed new models and provided late-seventeenth- and early-eighteenth-century English gardens with statuary which has not lost any of its value.

Another major artist whose designs are still available in lead was the Scottish architect Robert Adam, who was also responsible for the design and internal decoration of Georgian buildings in London and country houses in England and Scotland. He designed mainly in a neoclassical style and made great use of ideas dating back to Roman antiquity. Pompeii and Herculaneum, where major excavations were carried out in his lifetime had revealed houses buried under lava or volcanic ash, were a major source of inspiration. This was how his design for a handsome lead vase in a more or less neoclassical style and known as the 'Adam vase', came to be created. Basically, it is an oval vase with vertical reeding and an elegant pedestal.

Any visitor to the garden of Sissinghurst Castle has seen the lead vases above the sunken grass path leading from the Yellow Garden by the Priest's House to the herb garden. They are placed on a brick wall and surrounded by climbing plants such as *Clematis viticella* 'Alba',

Iron étagères for pots are available in many shapes and sizes. It all depends on what you do with them: is your étagère to become a chaotic mixture of forms, or will you create an entity by arranging one type of plant on it?
(Design by Jacques Wirtz, Izegem.)

The greens, the greys of the stone statue, and the dark colour of the water combine to 'neutralize' the white obelisks and make them look like illuminated stone waterfalls.
(Private garden in Shropshire.)

These 'flat' sundials are often to be seen in Britain, but also elsewhere: a triangle on a north–south axis casts lines of shadow on a stone dial, making it possible to tell the time. (Wespelaar Estate near Haacht in Belgium.)

with its delicate white bell-shaped flowers swaying round the grey of the lead. Many lead models are still cast in England and exported to various countries.

Pots

In the warm countries surrounding the Mediterranean, pots have a different purpose from that in northern Europe. Plant pots, particularly those made of terracotta, are used as containers either for plants needing a great deal of water, or for those needing to be placed in sheltered positions during the winter.

Hydrangeas are among the moisture-loving plants that people like to have in Italian and Spanish gardens. By planting them in pots, they can be watered more effectively without the moisture being wasted in the soil. A dish is sometimes placed under the pot to prevent the water draining away.

The other reason – the ability to move delicate plants around – is not an unnecessary luxury in countries such as Italy. Snow fell in many parts of the country in recent winters, and the Mediterranean coast of

France is regularly struck by frost. It is therefore essential to be able to move small orange, lemon and pomegranate trees, as well as many other favourite plants, indoors if frost is forecast.

The need to cultivate certain plants in pots led to a particular kind of garden layout. In many Italian renaissance and baroque gardens, small columns on which to place pots are erected in between the cypress or box hedges. The orange or lemon trees in their pots are placed on the columns and add form to the often severe symmetry of the garden.

From Italy, the use of pots spread all over Europe centuries ago. More recently, many people were inspired by what they saw in Spain and France and brought pots home with them after their holidays. In the Netherlands, for instance, very large terracotta pots were unknown until about ten years ago, when the first large Spanish specimens containing rubber plants, olives or bougainvilleas arrived there. These were simple pots, wide at the top and narrow at the bottom, with minimal ornamentation. Now, however, the market is flooded with richly decorated models which are sometimes very beautiful but may also seem rather too fussy.

Why not start off with some original planting for the pots you already have? Their majestic elegance renders any further addition superfluous.
(The Old Rectory, Burghfield, Berkshire.)

It is well known that pots are ideal plant containers for standing on a terrace, by the front door, or by a seat somewhere in the garden. Pots are often arranged symmetrically to give a dual sense of tranquillity and robustness. The fact that this is not a hard and fast rule becomes evident as soon as one suddenly feels tired of symmetry and starts pushing them around.

Animals as garden ornaments

The primeval strength associated with lions has always appealed to people representing power or seeking it. That is why lions were chosen to symbolize cities such as Venice, where a lion on top of a marble column in St Mark's Square towers above the city. Lions flanking steps up to buildings also act as custodians for powerful human beings.

In its simplest form, something of that concept is still to be found in our garden culture. One example is the lion's head on sale in lead, bronze or terracotta as a fountainhead. In days gone by, the water pouring out of its mouth from the supply pipe must surely have imparted some of its strength to those who drank it.

Now, however, we regard the lion's head merely as a handsome object and are no longer quite so sensitive to symbolism or so interested in displaying our power. At least, so we think, but in every period or change of circumstances, people still seek ways of displaying their wealth or authority. Certain breeds of dogs, for instance, have now become a status symbol or a sign of wealth, though such generalizations may be somewhat rash.

Sculptures of dogs, often in recumbent positions, can be seen in old gardens, and fortunately also in new ones. Magnificent gun dogs and greyhounds carved in stone once again guard the entrances to houses or steps leading up to them. Fortunately, they are also copied in Chilstone, Haddonstone and terracotta, and therefore available to all.

I am the owner of a greyhound made of white marble aggregate, which is at least 1½ yards (1.40 metres) tall, a little too white, and totally impossible to place. It is too white for the garden and too conspicuous for indoors. I am, however, still hoping to create a corner for

This lion has been silently roaring for centuries in the garden of Jenkyn Place, Bentley in Hampshire. The shade and large amount of greenery here create an atmosphere to which the ornament lends an imperious touch.

it in my new garden amid white gravel, bulbs, pointed yew trees and an ivy-covered arch ...

The best positions for the rather grey, sand-coloured dogs produced by Chilstone or Haddonstone are on either side of terraces, back doors or steps. Or they can be placed by a seat intended as a focal point. They look well with a few pots of ivy or other trailing plants at their feet. If they are rubbed over with buttermilk, they soon acquire a slightly greenish colour and begin to look like centuries-old garden antiques from a grand family estate.

I often choose seats as ornaments as there is something obvious and natural about them. Surely it ought to be possible to sit in a garden?
Here, in Claartje de Gruyter's garden, is a copy of the seat that Lutyens designed for Vita Sackville-West.

Avenues, Paths and Entrances

A tree-lined avenue leading up to a house is a favourite introduction to all the beauty soon to be revealed. 'Never show off,' is a wise saying which English and American gardeners interpret as meaning that the garden's best-kept secrets should never be revealed at the entrance. A great deal should be left to guess at, all the more reason for making the entrance to a house or garden tranquil and unfussy.

A peaceful entrance with trees

Creating shade is one way of giving an entrance a calm and relaxed atmosphere. Trees lining a path soon give it a dark and slightly mysterious quality. Foliage plants such as hostas, ferns and all varieties of geranium can grow in the shade there. Box will not do well, nor will yew, holly or Christmas roses. Grass will thrive only if some light is allowed to penetrate the foliage. Yet grass growing near a shady entrance looks calming and luxurious, and will thus create an important illusion of relaxation. The famous Katsura Villa in Japan teaches us how to prepare guests for a visit.

The waiting pavilion at the Katsura Villa

Anyone visiting Prince Toshihito was first thoroughly prepared before being received at his magnificent villa. Toshihito, who was born in the sixteenth century, rightly believed that guests should be given an opportunity to calm down and prepare themselves for the meeting with their host.

A special pavilion was built for the purpose. It contained three seats so arranged that people were never obliged to look other invited guests straight in the eye. The rule was to let visitors wait there for a quarter of an hour before they were admitted: fifteen minutes of contemplation, composing themselves, and pondering about the essence of what they wished to achieve in the course of the visit.

The European equivalent

What kind of European equivalent is there for the pavilion at the Katsura Villa? Our West-European gardens provide a number of opportunities. Create a space, preferably covered, for a seat immediately

Photograph on pages 62/63: *Pruned trees such as these* Catalpas *indicate that the spot, the avenue or the path belongs to the house. On leaving their cars, Jacques Wirtz takes visitors along this clipped avenue to the turning on the right of the ornament which leads up to the front door.*

André Eve's garden (Jardin des Roses Anciennes at Pithiviers) in autumn, full of species and varieties of ancient roses. The path meanders along, and to the left and right of it there are masses of more or less identical plants with a few breaks in the continuity...

beyond the parking area. Add a few shiny-leafed plants such as *Bergenia* and *Camellia* to attract the eye and encourage the visitor to relax. Provide some rustling plants, bamboo for instance, which will calm the mind. Introduce an element of water, preferably almost or entirely invisible, which will have the same effect. Arrange the small seating area in such a way that people are drawn towards it almost automatically. It might include a small statue or a few pots of simple annuals such as *Heliotrope* or white ivy-leafed pelargoniums.

How delightful it would be if it were to become customary here to allow our guests a few minutes' peace and quiet in that kind of a spot before inviting them into the house. A tray with glasses and a jug of iced water on it ... and a relaxed guest would arrive at the front door.

Creating an avenue leading up to the house might provide another means of allowing guests a few moments of peace before entering the house. This would have a similarly calming effect and provide a brief respite from everyday anxieties. The rhythm of the trees, the path itself, the clear outlines of the shadows or, in winter, the pattern of branches above one's head – all these elements generate a kind of restful atmosphere in which to prepare for the visit.

Unfortunately, not every house provides an opportunity for creating a long avenue leading up to it, and we must therefore look for substitutes. One of them is an entrance planted all over with trees. A green canopy is restful and invites contemplation, unlike a front garden full of ornaments, pots of flowers and bright roses. That may well be exciting, but in a shady garden all is calm and modest, with no more than, say, two pots of white busy Lizzies. There might also be one or two seats inviting guests to rest a while before proceeding to the front door.

In this garden (owned by Claartje de Gruyter in Vught), I had groups of four or two Catalpas *planted at the transitions between the individual garden 'rooms'. They contrast well with the yew hedges.*
The blue Hosta glauca *'Robusta' is planted in front of the* Miscanthus.

Paths in the garden itself – a calming feature

Having dealt with the guests, how about the host or hostess? How can they find peace? Monks and nuns used to stroll in their cloisters to read their breviaries or to pray as they passed along the columns supporting the roof built over their walkway. Breviaries were also read beyond the cloisters, in splendid avenues cut through forests or specially planted to induce tranquillity. Walking among trees is clearly restful and allows the mind to concentrate or relax, an important reason for planting long or short avenues in gardens.

The very idea of planting an avenue in the gardens of most home owners would seem ridiculous in view of the lack of space. Yet two rows of four fruit trees, ball-shaped acacias or maples will have a similar effect.

Trees such as limes can be pruned to form an avenue that need not be at all long. A similar effect can be achieved with other trees, hornbeam (*Carpinus betulus*) for instance, which are not commonly used for this particular purpose. There is a beautiful example in the garden of Hidcote Manor in the Cotswolds, which makes one wonder why the effect of its delicate young leaves and easily pruned branches is not copied more often. We are obviously more bound by tradition than we care to admit. It is not generally known either that beech (*Fagus sylvatica*) can also be pruned and trained to form espaliers for a short avenue. Beech espaliers look particularly good in winter, with their withered leaves faded to shades of brick red and brown.

For anyone with space, there is a choice of all kinds of trees. The Belgian landscape architect Jacques Wirtz often chooses hornbeam on stems for the long straight avenues that feature regularly in his garden designs. Sometimes they form two rows lining a simple path made of boulder clay, thus creating the impression of an avenue.

If they are not long enough, stately avenues often seem to me rather gloomy and pretentious. I therefore prefer white-flowered cherries (*Prunus yedoensis*), ornamental apples (white-flowered *Malus*) such as *Malus floribunda*, or fruit trees for simple avenues.

Sometimes, however, I also design short avenues of bog oak because the horizontal branches of this tree, which also thrives on dry or normal soil, have fresh green leaves which glisten in the rain or the sunshine. The leaves of this kind of oak turn red in autumn and look quite spectacular.

Lovers of small leaves choose birch, particularly for sandy soils. The equally delicate leaves of *Gleditsia* allow a soft light to penetrate; the pattern of its branches creates a somewhat Japanese effect. This is also true of the native acacia, *Robinia pseudoacacia*. The branches reaching for the skies have fantastic outlines and grow out of beautifully grooved trunks which in old age acquire a decorative value of their own.

For years I have been for regular walks along an avenue of white poplars in the Dutch province of North Holland. There is something wild and unforgettable about an avenue of that kind. The leaves are silvery white underneath and grey on top. As there always appears to be a gale blowing, a walk past these trees presents a tumultuous spectacle of silvery-grey colours. In winter the leaves are black, which is also a remarkable sight. The white poplar has a major drawback though: the branches of old trees are apt to break off, thereby creating a rather chaotic appearance.

A old farmhouse called 'Heuvelhof'
B black-tarred wooden barn of the Zeeland type
C formal yellow and white flower garden
D paved area in front of the farmhouse
E front door
F medieval flower garden with holly hedges
G grass path enclosed within beech hedges
H knot garden with low herb hedges
I terrace
J pond, formerly the cesspit
K herb garden
L drinking pool for cattle
M borders with poisonous plants and long canal
N maze
O nut trees forming avenues and squares
P avenue of apple trees and marguerites
Q holly hedges
R native flowers

I bought this piece of land at the end of 1992 and was inspired by the old farmhouse to lay out a medieval garden. Two types of avenue were planted in the large meadow: a long avenue with rows of nut trees (eight varieties) and an avenue of standard apple trees. New avenues now include a medlar avenue, a mulberry, pear and pollarded-willow avenue. It has almost turned me into an avenue fanatic.

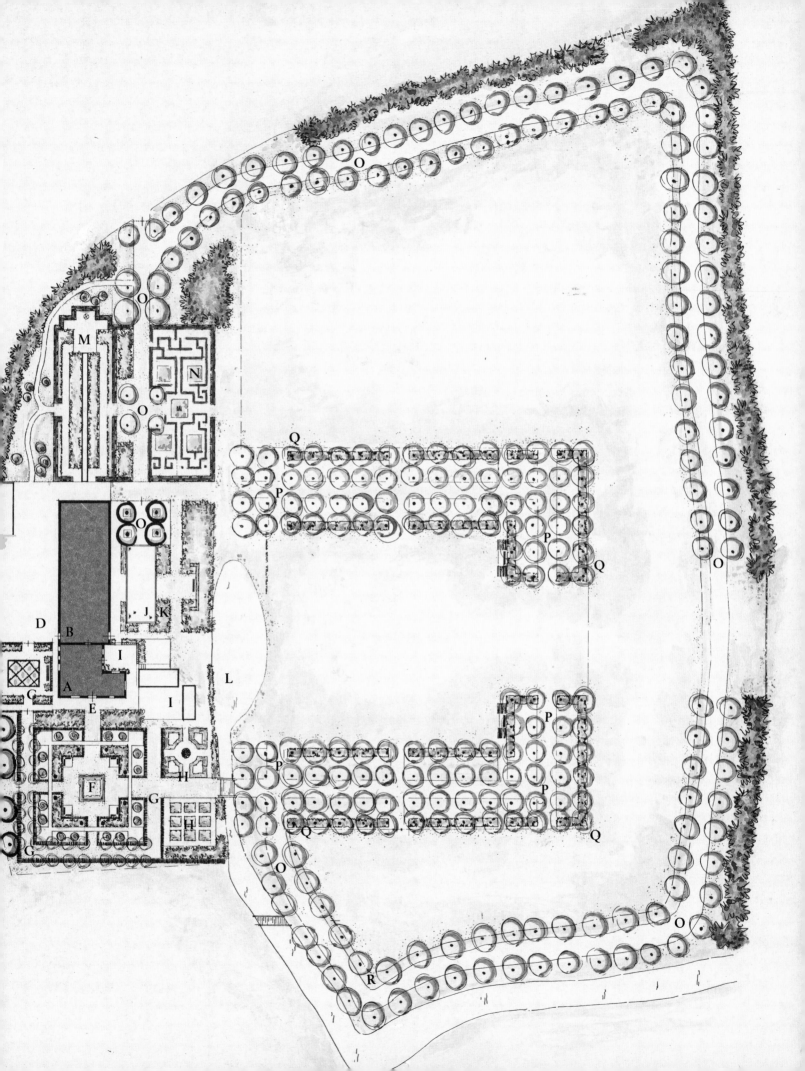

Hornbeam, Carpinus betulus, is usually grown as a hedge; this illustration shows that it can be used equally well to form avenues and hedges on slender trunks. (Design by Jacques Wirtz.)

Aspen is not grown often enough, despite the fact that this tree can provide so much musical pleasure. Its rustling leaves can drive away our thoughts and so lead to relaxation and musical enjoyment.

Many trees are splendid for creating original avenues: go and take a look at large houses on country estates, or walk through a tree nursery where all the young trees are planted in rows. This should lead to some new ideas for developments which are not yet to be seen everywhere. Be bold enough to make your own choice when planning an avenue.

Lovers of tradition, however, will never let this plea deflect them from planting oaks, beeches or limes to achieve a wonderful 'old-fashioned' avenue with its mentally calming effect.

It is obvious that avenues are highly symmetrical, and anyone intending to grow one will first envisage equidistant planting on both sides. This, however, is not necessary, and more imaginative symmetry can also be achieved.

Imaginative symmetry at De Wiersse

Major Gatacre and his wife Alice de Stuers spent a long time considering and discussing their plan to plant an avenue. They wanted to give the avenue leading up to their small country-house type of castle with its large and now world-famous garden an exciting landscaped appearance rather than a stiff and formal one. Several basic ideas had to be incorporated.

Firstly, they wanted the avenue to be very long and straight. Secondly, the type of tree had to be native oak (*Quercus robur*). Thirdly, the avenue would have to end at the castle. Fourthly, the avenue's surroundings, which consist of large meadows, had to be made part of the walk along the avenue. Beyond the meadows there is a wood of mixed oaks and beeches.

Major Gatacre envisaged a scenic entity, which meant that the distance between the trees should not be the same all along the avenue. By varying the distances, he would be able to create both wide and restricted views of the meadows. This simple scheme can be admired at De Wiersse, where the extensive park and many specialized gardens are open to the public three times a year.

If these ideas are considered in relation to small gardens, it will be evident that the effect of an avenue can be achieved without having

*At Planbessin in Normandy, this grass
avenue in the garden belonging to Monsieur
and Madame Sainte-Beuve leads to a quiet
pond. The rounded tops of these two* Catalpa
bungei *contrast with all the straight lines.*

In Corrie Poley's garden at Nisse in the Dutch province of Zeeland, the narrow path emphasizes the luxuriant growth of the geraniums, Centranthus *and white roses which form an entity with the cobbles in the circle.*

Grass paths form welcome breaks, particularly where plants are no longer very interesting after they have finished flowering, or in winter. They are also pleasant to walk on. (Barrington Court in Somerset.)

to resort to a fully symmetrical subdivision of a road, garden path or grass walk. An asymmetrical grouping of trees is equally possible and constitutes a kind of imaginatively symmetrical accompaniment to the path or walk.

The glorious Catalpa

Catalpa bignonioides is the botanical name of the bean tree. This general favourite, however, is subject to a number of tricks.

In Claartje de Gruyter's garden, *Catalpas* were chosen to provide rhythm and become striking features at the transitions between the individual garden 'rooms', where they presented the appearance of large green parasols. Two trees were always placed opposite each other at the spot where one had to walk in between them. After a few years, we found that the trees grew into beautiful shapes in sheltered positions. Needless to say, that satisfactory development also led to a problem: the trees spread out and now require regular pruning. Even so, the extensive annual growth is always a delight to behold as the large oval light-green leaves catch the light so beautifully and thus form a contrast with the dark-green yew hedges.

Catalpa bignonioides 'Aurea'

All *Catalpas* can be pruned severely and it is even possible to pollard them. This is often seen in Belgium, where they are planted symmetrically at the entrances to houses. Annual pruning keeps the trees in shape and under control, while retaining the rhythm of the many trunks. The 'Aurea' variety of *Catalpa bignonioides* has yellow leaves. It is an interesting tree for a gloomy patio, or a terrace, or near a dark thatched house or a boring post-war one in need of some drama. And if the back of your garden suggests nothing but doom and gloom, a bush of this golden shrub may provide relief. Plant some evergreen ferns and large foliage plants such as *Gunnera* round it, and this beautiful focal point will dispel any suggestion of melancholy.

An ornamental garden has been planted in the old kitchen garden of Upton House, north-west of Banbury, Warwickshire. There is a long vista in between large groups of perennials forming a deliberate entity, undisturbed by individual plants. A pleasing serenity is thereby achieved.

Catalpa bungei

Until some ten years ago, this ball-shaped variety of the *Catalpa* family was scarcely known. Now it is a major feature in garden design. As a substitute for the ubiquitous ball-shaped acacia, the large-leafed *C. bungei* with its beautiful rounded shape is ideal on its own in a small garden or for planting extensively in large ones. Grow them along a path, or plant four trees overlooking a terrace – there are innumerable applications.

If the ball becomes too big, cut it back. Pollard it in such a way that a small new ball can appear in the course of the summer.

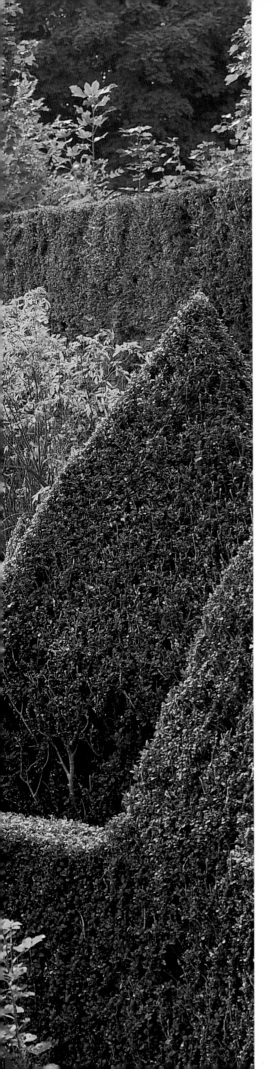

Box Hedges and Topiary

From father to son, members of the Mollet family looked after the French royal gardens in the sixteenth and seventeenth centuries, and first introduced *Buxus sempervirens* as a royal hedging plant.

As the person responsible for gardens such as those of the Louvre in Paris, Claude Mollet was always searching for low hedging plants which could survive the winter. Having frequently and expensively replaced miles of low hedges killed off by frost, he decided to look for a different hedging plant.

He chose box, first taking cuttings from the evergreen shrubs used as underplanting in the groves forming part of the royal gardens. When this proved successful and many thousands of plants had been cultivated, the box plants were planted out for the first time. The preparations had taken over five years.

Aristocratic garden owners actually regarded box as an inferior plant. Necessity, however, knows no law, so that Mollet was granted royal approval to plant the first box parterre. Other gardeners soon followed his example.

André Mollet, Claude's son, used box on a very large scale in the garden of Prince Frederick Henry of Orange at Honselaarsdijk in the Netherlands. This travelling member of the family of French royal gardeners had been invited to design two parterres at the Dutch palace belonging to the Prince and his wife, Amalia van Solms. Mollet incorporated box, grass, marble and other coloured stone chippings in them. One parterre was embellished with a topiary lion of Holland and the other with handsome box garlands. Although nothing is left of the palace, there are fortunately many engravings showing the garden and Mollet's two parterres.

Box is firmly established in our gardens

Box has an air of mysticism about it. At one time, small branches of box were suspended over fireplaces and in stables at Easter to bring luck to man and beast. This ancient custom is still observed in a few places.

Box twigs were sometimes planted near a farm or by the town or village hall. The cuttings took root and large box trees developed everywhere. They could be clipped into forms such as balls, points, peacocks and chickens. The fact that they were very easy to prune explains why these evergreen, originally Mediterranean shrubs became so popular in gardens for hedging and other purposes.

It is often thought that box does not grow tall, but that is not so.
In the garden of Birr Castle in Ireland, there is an avenue of more than
33-foot (10-metre) tall large-leafed *Buxus rotundifolia*. There are fast and
slow-growing varieties of box. *B. sempervirens* is the one that will be
offered for sale in nine out of ten cases, which is a pity. *B. rotundifolia* is
strong, handsome, decorative and can grow into very tall topiary trees
or unpruned bushes, if that is preferred.

Box can be planted to form many handsome patterns, as the
Mollet family discovered as early as the seventeenth century. This art
continues to fascinate people, and original applications are to be found
all over the world. Mathematical patterns were popular in renaissance
gardens, where a square was often placed diagonally inside another
square.

Similar designs can be found in many pattern books published at
the time of the Mollets. One of them is the splendid Jardin de Plaisir,
by André Mollet. Jan van der Groen, Dutch gardener to William III,
wrote an equally attractive book with patterns for the layout and maintenance of gardens. Such patterns could still be used as sources of
inspiration to enliven our current repertoire. There is more about this
in the chapter on mosaics.

Box is used with great inventiveness in the United States. The
bushes are sometimes combined with grey-leafed, or red or gold-
coloured herbs to create knot gardens. These were first developed in
the days of Elizabeth I. In the United States, the knots are made of
herbs such as lavender, thyme, *Artemisia* and *Santolina*, while *Teucrium*
is another shrub that is frequently used.

Box topiary

The Netherlands have a great tradition in creating topiary.
Though the ideas mainly originated in Italy and subsequently in
France, the art of pruning and training was perfected and kept alive in
the Netherlands. Even today, a new craze for shaping box and other
evergreen shrubs and conifers has developed.

At the time of William and Mary in the late-seventeenth century,
there were vast exports of clipped box peacocks, spirals, chickens and
the like from Holland to England, where people had not yet become
very interested in devoting years to creating these topiary forms. Box

A corridor in an impressive town
   house overlooking one of the canals
   in Amsterdam
B terrace, large pink and light-grey
   paving slabs, 20 x 20 in (50 x 50 cm)
C broderie of box
D blue-leafed Hosta
E box spirals, nearly 6 foot
   (2 metres) tall
F large-leafed Hosta
G perennials and tall shrubs such as
   lilac and holly
H a rose pergola
I sundial
J seat on a terrace paved with
   clinker bricks
K hydrangea
L summerhouse with the office of the
   Nederlandse Tuinenstichting
   (Netherlands Garden Foundation)
M two statues on plinths
N adjoining garden described on
   page 56
O pink roses

The Prins Bernard Fonds (Prince
Bernard Fund), which grants subsi-
dies, has its office in a grand canalside
house in Amsterdam. The Nederlandse
Tuinenstichting (Netherlands Garden
Foundation) occupies the summer-
house. Between the two buildings
there is a beautiful garden, designed
by the architect Rooyaerds and slightly
altered by me. Roses and blue-leafed
hostas were planted in the box-edged
bed to replace the original red and
white begonias. A border was created
and large numbers of hydrangeas
were planted in it.
The box spirals in this elegant yet
dramatically beautiful garden are
quite unique.

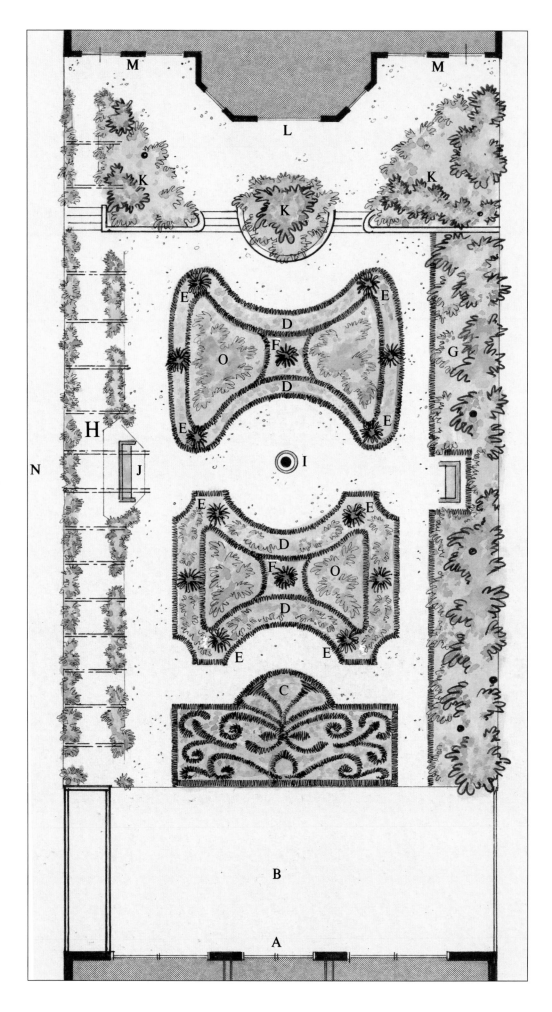

as well as yew remained popular in France for adding vertical touches to parterres. Points and spirals were the shapes that were cultivated most frequently.

Topiary trees can grow huge. Besides those in the garden of Birr Castle, there are magnificent examples in the United States, such as the giant topiary yews in the Du Pont gardens at Longwood in Pennsylvania... Everest Miller, the landscape architect responsible for these renowned show gardens and greenhouses, told me that he had managed to buy them when a small nursery on Long Island closed down. It was a real stroke of luck, since these topiary sculptures require decades of devoted care and they are therefore almost beyond price these days.

Topiary in contemporary gardens

It is widely recognized that curves look attractive in present-day gardens. A round shrub will soon grow into a more or less conical shape. Topiary trees are even to be found in ultra-modern gardens because they can be such handsome architectonic features. Placed in suitable positions, they will fit in with either modern or traditional schemes to form islands of tranquillity on wintry days when plants are probably not at their best or have disappeared altogether.

Anyone in need of inspiration should take a look at the garden of Walenburg Castle. There, handsome yew points are the sole example of topiary apart from the hedges of which they form part. Six tall yew points, over 9 foot (3 metres) tall, stand like lookouts at the beginning or end of each hedge, depending on the position of the viewer. Their height makes them handsome pivotal points for anyone entering or leaving the garden.

One of the first people to grow topiary balls on a large scale was Arie Dekker, who planted a whole series of round box trees by the terrace of her large modern garden in Zeeland. Over the years they have grown into very fine specimens. The row of trees forms an architectonic transition between the modern house and the large garden; it creates a haven of tranquillity and also of support in winter when all the perennials have died down.

Cultivating box

Anyone who grows box will need to trim the plants. It is easy to take cuttings from the twigs that have been removed, and they can be given away, sold or planted in the garden.

I have adopted a simple method of striking cuttings. I dig over an area of garden which is shaded by a shrub, and break up any large lumps of soil. I then put all the largish cuttings in the ground and pull off some of the lower leaves from them, so that none of them is in contact with the soil.

Right: *All kinds of grey-leafed plants have been brought together in this private garden at Planbessin in Normandy. In the foreground:* Artemisia 'Powis Castle' *and* lavender; *on the left:* Salvia purpurea. *On the far right above the seat:* Pyrus salicifolia, *also grey, with clumps of* Artemisia. *In between them, box balls rest the eye and guide it towards a couple of focal points.*

Left: *The 'Dutch Garden' was popular in England at the time of William and Mary in the late seventeenth century. The garden at Levens Hall near Kendal in Cumbria has been kept in that style, though the topiary has now rather outgrown its surroundings.*

Below: *Gertrude Jekyll designed the garden of Barrington Court in Somerset. Not only did she devote attention to topiary and lovely flowering plants, but her expertise is also apparent in the patterns of the brick paving.*

It is best not to choose very young cuttings. If you look carefully, you will find that some of them have a piece of greyish wood at the bottom. This is wood that was formed last year. If at all possible, make sure you use only the cuttings with a piece of old wood at the foot. They root well and tend not to dry out or rot, as so often happens to cuttings with growth developed only in the year of pruning. If you do wish to plant completely green cuttings, then it is best to use a rooting powder, which is obtainable from garden centres. If you have a small greenhouse, grow the cuttings in soil under a piece of plastic sheeting to prevent them drying out. Water all cuttings in times of drought and then you will be unlikely to lose any.

Creating topiary is sometimes simple and sometimes less so. Balls, points and cubes are easy; spirals and baskets – not to mention animals and other hollow shapes – are more difficult.

The intended shape is sometimes preformed in wire, a skill which is quite easy to learn if you are prepared to take some trouble. You will need strong wire, still just flexible, which can be allowed to rust in due course. Take long straight pieces and assemble them over the plant. The box tree is left to continue growing, but any shoots projecting beyond the iron framework are trimmed. If a broad shape is required, one or more twigs should be tied to the wire to make them grow in the right direction. Pruning twice a year is more than enough for box. Topiary as a hobby will give a great deal of pleasure to anyone who has discovered it!

One problem facing people who grow their own topiary is that the garden will eventually begin to look like a collection of curiosities. There are two possible solutions: you either plant anything that is not in keeping with your layout in pots and embellish terraces with them, or else you pass on whatever you have left over to new enthusiasts.

Left: *In the garden of Lower Hall, Worfield, Shropshire, the striking colours of the brick paving are repeated in those of the flowering shrubs. The shape of the box topiary is reassuringly simple.*
(Source: Gardens of England and Wales, 1994 ed.)

The planting scheme at Powis Castle in Wales is among the finest in Britain. Four large green topiary trees have been planted in the grass to provide visual support to the ornamental feature.

The Kitchen Garden and the Flower and Vegetable Garden

The kitchen garden – the functional part of all the different types of garden that have developed thus far – has probably remained closest to its original form and appearance. Walled or hedged vegetable gardens are to be seen in woodcuts, paintings as well as in old herbals and gardening books. They are the primordial gardens, since gardens for growing vegetables existed before mankind had reached the stage of creating ornamental gardens with fountains, flowers and statuary.

Human beings have always felt the need for plants and fruit that could be harvested. They gathered fruit in their habitat by searching across open country, in forests, along river banks and on hillsides. This must sometimes have been a protracted task, especially when people began to gather more and more livestock around them. As the animals sometimes ate the same plants and fruit as humans, it was essential to fence in areas of land. Fences consisted either of wattle made of branches woven into branches inserted in the ground, or of branches placed close together. Walls were built by daubing mud on to wattle consisting of branches and twigs. In areas near rivers, the walls of houses were constructed in exactly the same way. Stone was used for making walls wherever it was abundant. Magnificent examples are still to be seen in unspoilt rural areas in France, England, Wales and Scotland. The stones had to be removed from fields and were piled up around them to form walls. The enclosed gardens could be filled with all the tuberous and other plants, including fruit-bearing shrubs and trees, that provided something edible for human beings.

The earliest depictions of gardens known to us are very rudimentary and it was not until the Middle Ages that clear European illustrations were produced which give us an idea of how a vegetable garden was laid out. There was often a path down the centre, with other paths along the sides. Depending on the size of the garden, there were also paths dividing the garden crossways and lengthways into sections that were easier to maintain.

This kind of functional division always included a strongly symmetrical element. Perhaps that was due to the Roman method of intersecting towns and land by means of roads. It may also be the result of practical considerations: subdividing the kitchen garden mathematically leads to easy maintenance.

Be that as it may, symmetrical schemes have always played a major part in kitchen gardens. As a result of the required crop rotation, the planting of the individual sections was scarcely symmetrical at all. Crop rotation is essential for preventing soil exhaustion and the risk of

Photograph on pages 84/85: *Annuals for cut flowers are now sown where vegetables were once cultivated. It makes a bright and cheerful sight.*
(Private garden in Normandy.)

Fruit trees are part of a kitchen garden, sometimes to cover walls, elsewhere to provide a row of trees or, as at Heale House, not far from Salisbury in Wiltshire, a pergola of apples. With perennials planted in front of the trees, the utility garden has been turned into an ornamental one.

disease. If vegetables were to be grown in the same spot year in year out, there is a likelihood of soil exhaustion as a result of plants continuing to extract the same kinds of nutrients from it. Soil fatigue can therefore be prevented by growing the plants in a different section of the vegetable garden every year. Similarly, if the vegetables are grown in the same place every year, insects, moulds and viruses are given an opportunity to increase to such an extent that they ultimately begin to constitute a threat to such plants.

These are two good reasons for practising crop rotation and choosing a different spot for a particular crop every year. Crop rotation usually prevents growing plants symmetrically in the kitchen garden, but that does not stand in the way of the opportunity to devise a handsome symmetrical layout.

Fruit trees in the kitchen garden

Ever since the Middle Ages, monastic establishments have encompassed not only large kitchen gardens, but also orchards, pastures for animals, and sometimes even arable fields for corn, beet and so forth, as well as herb gardens. This pattern of growing everything that the occupants might require is also to be found on farms and the estates of castles and large country houses.

Many old-established kitchen gardens include fruit trees and, even more often, fruit bushes. Sometimes, if the kitchen garden is walled, there are fruit cordons, while elsewhere there are small clipped fruit bushes, and sometimes a few large fruit trees in between the soft fruit. In the *potager du roi* belonging to Louis XIV, fruit and vegetables were grown side by side.

A kitchen garden for a palace

There should be a campaign to restore not only the pleasure gardens, but specifically also the kitchen gardens belonging to historic buildings such as palaces, castles and houses that are open to the public. Too much emphasis is currently placed on ornamental gardens, as that is considered the way to attract visitors. Yet, anyone who has seen the engravings of the William and Mary kitchen gardens at, for instance, the palace of Het Loo, will be disappointed to find that, unlike the ornamental gardens, the kitchen gardens remain unrestored.

Looking back at the same apple pergola at Heale House (see previous pages), one can see the walls intended to keep deer, rabbits and hares away from the juicy vegetables growing luxuriantly behind the borders of flowers.

It is still possible to gain a good impression of this kind of complex in the kitchen garden of Louis XIV, the present Parc Balbi to the south of the palace of Versailles. Once the garden had been laid out at the rear of the palace, and many thousands of labourers had started work on the upkeep of this immense area, a new scheme was begun. To the south of the orangery and the orangery garden, there was a swamp, a malodorous area with excessive numbers of mosquitoes that used to annoy the royal family. It was therefore decided that the swamp should be eliminated; in fact, part of it was excavated and another part was raised up to a level where it was possible to turn it into a kitchen garden. The lake was named *La pièce d'eau des Suisses*, which is a reference to the members of the regiment of Swiss Guards who excavated the swamp.

The kitchen garden or *potager du roi* was laid out by Jean-Baptiste de la Quintinye, an enthusiast who made a great success of it. A bronze statue of him still stands on the raised northern terrace built

above the caves where agricultural produce could be stored at cool temperatures.

A system of walls was constructed round the huge kitchen garden. Espaliered apple and pear trees were planted against the wall. The central area was left open for vegetable gardens and divided into large sections by the principal paths. Several water reservoirs or ponds with stone borders were constructed at their intersections. Low, vertically trained fruit trees, including apples, line the main paths. They consist of just one branch which has been trained horizontally, giving a linear effect along the paths. Behind them, vegetables are still cultivated. Anything not used privately is auctioned and thus helps to cover a small part of the huge expenses incurred in pruning fruit trees, hoeing paths, fertilizing, digging, planting and harvesting. Fortunately, students from the nearby horticultural college are required to work in the garden, otherwise it would be impossible to meet the maintenance costs. It is a pity that so few other countries follow this example!

A hedge of apples like this one is trained along posts at an early stage. This form of fruit-growing is seen far too rarely nowadays. In renaissance and baroque vegetable gardens these low apple trees were often planted along paths. Here, the paths became grass, as did the vegetable beds, but the apples, which are grafted low down and trained horizontally at an early age, were kept as a reminder. It is something to try again, just like the arches with grapes and botanical roses trained over them instead of pears.
(Private garden near Fontainebleau.)

Combined flower and vegetable gardens

Farmhouses often have a section enclosed within a hedge or fence for growing vegetables and this is sometimes combined with a flower garden. Genuine working farms do not usually have a separate flower garden. After all, why not combine the two – it makes a difference to the amount of labour required if a single hedge enclosing a combined flower and vegetable garden is all that needs to be trimmed.

The way in which space is allotted to either flowers or vegetables varies from country to country, from region to region and even from village to village. I can remember a few fixed patterns from my own youth, when vegetables were often planted in the central section of an enclosed garden. In ancient kitchen gardens in England, however, I have often seen the reverse, with flowers along the centre path and vegetables beyond them.

Even today, many gardeners are experimenting with different combinations of flowers and vegetables, which have the advantage that there is then more to look at if the vegetable harvest should fail entirely.

Tinned vegetables, supermarkets and freezers have, on the other hand, made people wonder whether home-grown fruit and vegetables are not more expensive than shop produce. Unfortunately, that is frequently all too true, but more and more people like to grow their own vegetables in order to make sure that they have not been sprayed with chemicals. A combined flower and vegetable garden can make a welcome change from the traditional ornamental garden.

This impressive vegetable garden is to be found at the Old Rectory, in Burghfield, Berkshire. Grass paths are practical and look well in winter when most of the vegetables have died down. Crop rotation is ensured by moving the vegetables up one section each season.

Maintaining a kitchen garden, however, does not appeal to everyone. The discipline required for sowing, pricking out, hoeing, bedding out, pinching off tops and harvesting, all at the right time, is considerable. One can but admire born gardeners who tend their weedless, well-stocked kitchen gardens year in, year out. They are the true gardeners! As well as preserving the oldest form of gardening, they also eat well and keep fit.

A corridor with door to garden
B terrace with balustrade and pink-flowered roses and two grey-leafed Pyrus salicifolia
C pond with five conifer balls
D slope to raised summer house
E paving
F old-fashioned type of summer-house, now an office
G stone steps
H yew hedges
I terrace with pergola and grapes
J kitchen garden with box edgings
K two topiary peacocks
L two topiary bears
M pear cordons against an old wall
N summer-house
O water spout in wall over a brick basin
P white plants
Q trellis with roses
R entrance, door to garden from public highway
S henhouse and woodshed

The back of an impressive old town house in Haastrecht, the Netherlands, was designed in farmhouse style. There is a tall handsome summer-house at the back of the garden. I had a pond made, the lawn levelled, and all the left-over soil was used to construct a slope up to the summer-house. The slope was closely planted with shrubs, ivy and bush roses. Borders with pink, blue and grey-flowered perennials enclose the lawn. The colourful tall plants are themselves enclosed within yew hedges. On the right there is an ornamental vegetable garden with box hedges and topiary and a delightfully shady terrace. The summer-house where people eat and live in summer is properly roofed.

Flowers for cutting in the combined flower and vegetable garden

Any lover of flower arranging will always experience doubts about whether the ornamental garden visible from the house should be raided for this purpose. Flowers, after all, last much longer out of doors and, provided the spot where they are grown is carefully chosen, can be admired there just as well. There is a rather challenging solution to this problem: create a special garden for cut flowers.

If there is enough space, a garden for cut flowers can be laid out with enclosing hedges, separate divisions and a brick or grass path. The secret is to make it into a colourful entity. It is best to mix colours and not to turn it into yet another little garden laid out according to colour. Otherwise it would always be tempting to leave the flowers there so as not to spoil the beauty of the individual colours. So it is better to be multicoloured, with roses, perennials, dahlias and anything else that may be required for flower arrangements growing together in a bright and cheerful medley.

Anyone who does not much favour a separate garden for cut flowers and would prefer to combine it with a kitchen garden has equally good sense. It makes it possible to enliven the kitchen garden and plant it attractively. A combined vegetable and flower garden may even become so appealing that one puts a seat there or even creates a flowery arbour.

It is best to adhere to a symmetrical layout for this kind of combined flower and vegetable garden since that is most effective. As suggested above, plant anything you need in mixed beds. That does not necessarily mean that roses should be mixed with perennials, although it is permissible. In my own experience, however, roses do not care much for excessively wild undergrowth. So keep their feet clear or allow them to be overgrown by plants that are not too dense.

One further advantage of the combined flower and vegetable garden is that a home can be found there for dahlias, so many people's pet abomination. After all, there are some lovely varieties. Anyone visiting Powis Castle in Wales will find the most beautiful borders, seemingly always in flower, where dahlias have been cunningly planted in among the perennials, thus extending the flowering season until far into the autumn.

In the moderate climate of Normandy, Monsieur and Madame Sainte-Beuve created this large elegant herb garden at Planbessin. An old column forms the peaceful centre appropriate to a garden steeped in history. The grey and green colour scheme is repeated by the ornamental pear, Pyrus salicifolia, behind the seat.

There are several gardens near Bath (like this one at Claverton Manor), where a beehive is placed in the centre of the herbs. Creeping camomile grows round this feature, with box hedges to keep up its appearance in winter. Lemon balm, wild strawberries, chives and variegated mint grow in the densely planted bed in the foreground.

There are flowers for cutting in lovely colours and shapes, but it is necessary to go in search of them and not merely to plant familiar colours indiscriminately. Marguerites, phloxes, delphiniums, *Heliopsis*, *Thalictrum* and *Ligularia* undoubtedly belong to the cut flower collection. Choose plants which last well in vases and combine them with vegetables. Planted along the centre path or in broad strips along the sides of the vegetable garden, they provide a feast for the eyes. A further advantage is that they are inclined to curb vegetable diseases rather than encourage them!

Arches, cordons, pear-tree pergolas

Head gardeners – and usually the owners of gardens – were always proud of their kitchen gardens. They were quite willing to make a bit of a show of them. That is why simpler, but still quite attractive, methods were invented for embellishing a – usually rather flat – kitchen garden.

Sometimes, a pear-tree pergola was trained over a path, or several separate arches with apples, pears or apricots were placed across the paths. Elsewhere there are 'walls' of horizontal fruit-tree cordons along the principal paths, as there are in the kitchen garden of Barrington Court in Somerset.

There are other ways of embellishing the kitchen garden as well. Serpentine walls were a familiar sight in the Netherlands. The re-entrants in the rounded serpentine shape of the wall were very suitable for growing fruit cordons. There are about ten of those old Dutch walls left, now mostly listed as historical monuments.

The outbuildings belonging to old-established kitchen gardens are often equally fascinating. Like the grape houses, and the cold and heated frames, they are often beautiful functional types of fine simple architecture. They belong to the handsome kitchen garden, and anyone with enough time and money should aim to restore that tradition in the contemporary symmetrical kitchen garden.

Mosaics

Mosaics and patterns in the garden

Sixteenth- and seventeenth-century books on gardens include pages of patterns which can be introduced within rectangular or square beds. Many of those patterns are still quite usable today. They are usually geometrical divisions of the kind that everyone has been taught to draw with a ruler and dividers during mathematics lessons, and could easily design. There is an infinite interplay of straight lines and curves, sometimes combined and sometimes used separately to form a pattern or a subdivision of a garden or part of one.

Such patterns were obviously a major source of inspiration to garden designers as they endeavoured to achieve maximum diversity within the frame of a compartment. Contemporary examples of gardens laid out in patterns inspired by geometrical forms suggest that this idea is now prevalent again. Such gardens are sometimes inspired by earlier models, as happened at Pitmeddin in Scotland for example, but inventive minds may well design patterned gardens without being influenced in any way by historical precedent.

This phenomenon continues to fascinate me, and again and again I find myself drawing compartments which may include a pattern of hedges. It is not essential, however, to use only hedges for outlining a pattern. In the ornamental kitchen garden at the château of Villandry near the confluence of the Cher and the Loire, for instance, vegetables in various colours and shapes have been planted in sections to create striking mosaic effects. Red cabbage, curled endive, leeks, beetroot, chard and lettuces in a multitude of colours occupy one or more sections. The various combinations of sections have created original contrasting patterns that cannot be admired anywhere else. The vegetables are grown in a level area of the huge renaissance garden, which is itself divided into several parts. The whole of the ornamental vegetable garden is further divided into large sections separated from one another by paths. At the centre of their intersections, there are small fountains and ponds, with trellis arbours covered with red roses at the corners of the four converging sections. Each large square is planted and divided differently every year, thus preventing soil fatigue. The appearance of the vegetable garden therefore changes annually and always looks interesting.

To stress the symmetry of this kitchen garden mosaic, small pear trees have been planted and clipped into a conical shape. When in flower, they conceal the seasonal bareness of the vegetable patches, and also produce large quantities of pears later on.

Photograph on pages 96/97: *At Villandry, Dr Carvallo recreated a renaissance kitchen garden unequalled anywhere else in the world. The vegetable beds are edged with box and each bed is filled with one kind of vegetable.*

A contemporary mosaic can be created in this way with shades of blue, grey, yellow and green. Salvia officinalis 'Purpurascens' occupies the foreground; Santolina chamae-cyparissus *is grey and the box edgings are green. The yellow is created by the shrubs, an effect that may be achieved by golden box or golden privet.*

The garden of Villandry is a 'must' for all lovers of symmetry. The layout is entirely symmetrical and includes fascinating components such as a box and yew garden of love, edged beds of herbs, ponds with symmetrically placed waterspouts, steps, trees on slender trunks and so on. To think that Carvallo, a chocolate manufacturer with an interest in garden history, had this complex of gardens laid out at the beginning of the twentieth century! Just the repair of all the stone steps, walls and balustrades costs a fortune. This superior mosaic garden is certainly well worth a visit.

Ham House and the grey lavender and **Santolina** *mosaics*

In the seventeenth century, Lord Lauderdale, friend and adviser to King William and Queen Mary, lived at Ham House by the Thames in Surrey. From there he could travel to Hampton Court by boat to visit his sovereigns.

Lord Lauderdale was a typical seventeenth-century lover of culture, whose country house, miraculously still intact, was furnished in contemporary style. The area on the left of the garden is laid out as a parterre recently redesigned by Graham Thomas, the landscape architect who has refurbished so many National Trust gardens. Thomas decided on a mosaic-type layout. Various beds were hedged with box and planted with blue lavender and *Santolina*, a light-grey herb with yellow flowers. The combination of blue, grey, yellow and green has created an unforgettable sight.

It is doubtful whether this parterre looked the same in the days of Lord Lauderdale. In the seventeenth century people usually opted for more variety, as may be seen in the gardens of Het Loo, William and Mary's Dutch palace, which has now been restored.

Mosaics, a Victorian hobby

The abundance of seedlings which resulted when gardeners working in the second half of the nineteenth century began to sow annuals in greenhouses rather than out in the open had major consequences. What were the men to do with such huge quantities of young plants? The solution was as simple as it was brilliant: they were used to fill flower beds. Existing beds were cleared and, if they did not provide enough space, room for the annuals was found in the lawns. People

Rosemary Verey, the well-known writer and
gardener, designed this knot garden at
Barnsley House, not far from Cirencester.
The patterns date back to the days of
Elizabeth I and are formed here by green and
silvery box.

soon discovered that this created a jumbled impression and that the
overall effect looked much better if the plants were grouped according
to colour, or if at least the larger beds were restricted to a single shade.
The old sixteenth- and seventeenth-century patterns were revived, but
in the form of annuals combined with herbs such as rue (*Ruta grave-
olens*), with *Santolina*, lavender and all kinds of sedums and semper-
vivums. Grey-leafed plants became particularly popular for providing
extra colour in between the green leaves of the annuals before these
came into flower.

Suitable colour combinations

As I mentioned previously, green and grey are suitable colours
for elegant and quite sophisticated mosaics. Lovers of colour, however,
may regard such a combination as far too pale and delicate. In the eyes
of many gardeners, blue, red, yellow, violet and orange flowers are
summery delights that they do not wish to forego. The average Dutch
front garden is ablaze with colour in summer, and not a single contrast
is avoided.

Few people restrict themselves to choosing only shades of pink,
mauve, blue and grey, or yellow, blue and white. Most of them want a
profusion of bright colours for the summer. In that case, it may be surprising to discover that remarkable effects may be achieved with mosaic patterns, and fortunately there are some gardens where such effects
can be studied.

The unique patterned garden at Pitmedden

The sunken garden to be seen at Pitmedden is a reconstruction of
a seventeenth-century parterre laid out by Sir Alexander Seton. It is
impressively located some miles north of Aberdeen.

In May each year, the four principal sections of the mosaic garden, which is subdivided by hedges clipped to perfection, are planted
with home-grown annuals. The National Trust for Scotland, the authority responsible for the property's upkeep, makes a point of stressing
the fact that all the thousands of annuals are grown from seed by
Pitmedden's industrious gardeners. Beautiful geometric patterns of
Buxus sempervirens have been created within the framework of yew
hedges and paths subdividing the four main sections, with a different

At the château of Villandry, situated by the River Cher, vegetable beds of ornamental cabbage have been laid out in a remarkably strong rectilinear pattern round a pool.

pattern in each section. These geometrical patterns are filled with red, orange, yellow, blue, white and pink annuals, and every year provide a different and unrivalled example of how lovely mosaic planting can be. Two huge herbaceous borders surrounding the mosaic garden are also planted according to a rhythmical design. Fountains and ornaments beside the two identical pavilions in the northern and southern parts of the garden add brilliant touches.

The herb mosaics at Sudeley Castle

In English history, the Tudor style is characteristic of the renaissance period culminating in the reigns of Henry VIII and Elizabeth I. Mosaic patterns became popular in gardens during that same time, and there cannot have been many gardens without a mosaic or knot garden.

Sudeley Castle in Gloucestershire has a good example of this type of renaissance garden. The herb garden is particularly fascinating, as it is situated below the windows of the rooms where Catherine Parr, Henry VIII's sixth wife, once lived. It has been preserved between two ancient yew pergolas resembling dark green sculptures and acting as walls to the herb garden. The castle forms the third side and the fourth consists of a grassy slope obscuring the view of other parts of the garden.

A pond enclosed by a graceful balustrade with stone capping has been situated in the centre of this enclosed space. A vast mosaic garden planted with herbs surrounds the pond. *Santolina*, thyme, sage, purple-leafed marjoram and rue are all grown in individual beds. Together, they form a pattern in shades of grey, blue, pink and green, which constitutes a refined and apparently authentic reproduction of the examples of garden art known to have been created at the time of the Tudors.

The vegetable garden at Villandry presents a wonderful interplay of straight lines from almost every angle, with the symmetrical design adding to its striking appearance.

A garden door of the landscape architects' office
B staircase leading to the roof garden
C shade-tolerant, partly evergreen planting with ivy ground cover
D large beech
E large mature pear tree which gives a lot of shade
F gravel
G stepping 'stones' made of paving bricks
H stone steps
I box-edged compartments
J entrance to summer-house

Those thinking of mosaic patterns for their own gardens have several options. As may be seen in my Amsterdam town garden, it is possible to create a mosaic of compartments, which I have edged with box. One type of plant can then be grown in each bed, such as lavender, sage, hyssop or annuals. A second possibility is to divide up a section into various shapes. A third option consists of creating a square, a rectangle or a circle in a strip of soil or grass, enclosing it within a small hedge and then planting the various colour sections within the larger bed. My city garden is made up of two parts: the mosaic garden by the two identical town houses at the back, and a wood-like ivy garden under a large beech, a maple and a pear tree which give too much shade for any other kind of planting. I say my garden is maintenance-free, and so it is – almost!

French mosaic gardens

All kinds of French towns and villages fortunately still have their original mosaic beds. It is just as if time had stopped – cotoneasters, potentillas and hypericums appear to be totally unknown to many French municipal gardeners. Instead of striving for 'modernism', they have remained true to their own traditions in their small and perfectly kept parks and public gardens. This means that innumerable visitors can still admire pretty little mosaic gardens from the raked paths and handsome grey seats.

Mosaic patterns have also been preserved in several large gardens, including the château at Angers in the department of Maine-et-Loire. The impressive renaissance château with its tall towers and donjons is situated in a tidy, formal garden. When the château was restored between 1950 and 1960, the garden with its geometrical patterns was also re-created.

Another, particularly fine example is the *potager du roi* forming part of Louis XIV's palace gardens at Versailles. Magnificent mosaic planting can also be seen in the large parterres on the left and right at the rear of the palace. Year after year, blue *Verbena* and other annual mosaic plants are grown there between pointed forms of *Taxus baccata*.

Flower beds with annuals arranged in mosaic patterns can also be admired in the gardens of the château at Rambouillet in the department of Seine-et-Oise, and in those of the château of Fontainebleau.

All these examples can be a source of inspiration for creators of contemporary gardens.

Steps

Steps have been a characteristic architectural feature since time immemorial. They are often placed symmetrically in relation to the buildings to which they lead or from which they depart. That is not so strange if it is borne in mind that, for centuries, Western European architecture was based mainly on the principle of a balanced and ordered method of designing elevations.

Greeks and Romans set the examples for generations of architects. Even now, steps rising symmetrically to the façades of buildings are associated with the classical ideals of beauty.

Steps by themselves are bare features. Their appearance can be softened and made less severe with climbers, hedges and flowering plants, and this effect can be reinforced by selecting opposing forms.

Round topiary flanking steps

A Sleeping-Beauty effect, with plants apparently overwhelming the architecture, is something that is not always wanted. People often wish to restrict the plants flanking steps and in front of the building to which the steps lead to a height they have specifically chosen for the purpose. The choice of a rounded form for the topiary adds a formal note and this may act as a transition between the building and the garden.

As was emphasized in the chapter on topiary, all kinds of conifers and shrubs are suitable for clipping into a rounded form. Privet, yew, laurel, box and aucuba are well known to be plants which may be somewhat dull and gloomy, but are also very sturdy and capable of surviving in windy, shady and even air-polluted environments. Even plants such as the grey-leafed *Eleagnus*, the pink-flowered *Escallonia*, variegated holly and *Camellia* can be forced into rounded shapes. This is obviously also true of other hedging plants such as hornbeam (*Carpinus*), common beech (*Fagus*), may, *Berberis* and dogwood.

There can be too much of a good thing, however, and too many round forms in one area tend to look ridiculous. It is therefore best to combine 'round' with 'flat' and 'loose', which will look interesting and to some extent natural.

Straight topiary flanking steps

Those who prefer uniformity to contrast will be inclined to clip shrubs and hedges planted alongside steps into straight forms. In countries such as Italy and France, a hedge is often planted on each side of a flight of steps. The sides of the steps are thus as it were flanked with greenery. This is less common in the Netherlands, where the sides are allowed to form part of the structure and are not covered in clipped greenery. Still, it is possible to achieve splendid effects if the sides are covered in plants and horizontally clipped hedges. I always remember the gardens at Versailles or Villandry as perfect examples of the special advantages that such double 'walls' of stone and greenery may provide.

This is not the only way of flanking a flight of steps, as is evident in the evergreen blocks which are clipped flat alongside steps. It may create a strong and powerful effect to cultivate two blocks of evergreen plants to border the steps. Yew, privet and many other plants are suitable for architectonic forms of this kind. It is effective to repeat these blocks of greenery elsewhere in the garden so as to create a link between the steps, the greenery alongside them, and the rest of the garden.

Loose plant forms flanking steps

Many varieties of plants look well growing freely alongside symmetrical steps. Winter-flowering prunuses (*Prunus subhirtilla*), for example, are highly suitable because of their airy, open growth, beneath which many low-growing plants are likely to thrive.

Nothofagus antarctica with its Japanese-looking, fantastic and more or less horizontal branches looks pleasing with modern houses. *Cornus florida* will let its horizontal branches grow outwards to fit in well with modern as well as older types of architecture.

These three shrubs are all deciduous and open, but they are also tall, so that they will more or less veil part of the architecture next to the steps with a green haze.

Those who want loose forms but not tall plants have a large choice consisting of all kinds of shrubs such as buddleias, evergreen *Escallonia*, decorative white-flowered *Ligustrum quihoui* and shrub roses.

Roses can be particularly long-flowering provided modern varieties are chosen. After a dazzling month, old-fashioned shrub roses usually do not flower again, a bonus being that they sometimes produce hips.

If single topiary trees are planted to the left and right of steps, it is possible to choose between a closed form and an open one on 'legs'. A closed form is suitable in the case of an extremely dominant flight of steps. A clipped open-structured shrub on 'legs' is preferable if one wants to enhance a somewhat lighter structure. The planting should be adapted to the chosen form.

For a house with a flight of steps leading to the garden, it is possible to combine an infinite variety of round or flat clipped forms and loosely structured forms. The actual planting of this kind of strip is often difficult, but it is rewarding if proper advantage is taken of the architecture adjoining the steps.

A symmetrical flight of steps elsewhere in the garden

The symmetry that exists between house and garden is such an historically determined fact in Western garden culture that in many cases it is taken as a matter of course to make the same choice when subdividing the garden. The lines of the building are then continued into the garden with straight lines at right angles to the frontage and to one another.

Steps can play a decisive part when it is a matter of choosing between a completely flat garden and one with differences in levels. Unfortunately, steps are often expensive to construct; otherwise we should prefer to build them of the same stone or brick as that of the buildings.

In a symmetrical garden, anyone wanting to introduce different levels will opt for a central flight of steps. The next problem is that of deciding whether to build monumental steps, simple and hardly noticeable steps, or a steep or even dramatic flight of steps.

The simpler the steps in a garden, the more successful they are likely to be, but in the case of large houses built in the late nineteenth or early twentieth century there are many examples of monumental flights of steps which are highly successful as well as appropriate. As our contemporary gardens are usually smaller and we are inclined to treat them more romantically and less severely, a simple flight is usually advisable. If there is still a need for formality and drama, it is possible to plant topiary balls, cubes, cones or, if need be, spirals near them. A rose-covered arch, two stone dogs or round balls, a few pots – all such aids will help to dramatize a flight of steps within a garden.

The Astilbe *flowers light up like small flames in the shady garden of Hodnet Hall in Shropshire. Imaginative symmetry is created where the repetition of similar forms and colour add rhythm to the long meandering path.*

What lies beyond the steps?

In old gardens one occasionally sees groves of mountainous rhododendrons growing beneath mature oak trees and together terminating the main axis and its flight of steps. It is hard to imagine anything lovelier.

Younger gardens rarely include such features, and alternatives need to be found for them. One solution might consist of espaliered lime trees with a hedge below them and a handsome seat in front. Another could be an herbaceous border with two box topiary trees or a terrace with pots and a small round table. A pergola, rose-covered arches – there is an infinite number of ways of creating an end to the principal garden vista.

There is a constant flow of new and easily assembled structures. Trellis looks fine with ivy and small-flowered clematis. Anyone considering a new focal point may be overhasty in deciding on an architectural feature and perhaps start building a handsome summer-house. Yet I would argue in favour of first trying to use plants for terminating the visual axis from a flight of steps. What could be more captivating than plants which are allowed to grow either freely or into solid shapes, or into a combination of the two?

Materials for constructing steps

Clay is a material which has been available to builders for centuries. Houses, walls, paths and roads have been constructed of bricks and clinker bricks made of baked clay. Their colour varies from region to region, depending on the river from which the clay was extracted.

Clay was taken from the nearest river and baked to form bricks – paving bricks took slightly longer. They were first used for the construction of buildings in the vicinity of the deposits and later used further afield. It is possible to tell by the colour of old buildings which river they must be near. Depending on their origin, the size of the bricks often varied as well. Rhine bricks, for example, are smaller than the clinker bricks made of clay from the River Waal. IJssel bricks, also named after the eponymous river, are small and yellow.

It is a fortunate circumstance that, formerly, people usually chose the same kind of bricks for constructing garden steps as had been used for their house, palace or country mansion. This created an almost natural harmony.

We might well hanker after such harmony in the latter days of the craze for railway sleepers and hardwood posts. As a result of using wood, there is no longer any link with the material of the house unless that too was made of timber.

There is an explanation for the fact that wood became so popular as an alternative to brick for building flights of steps. Depending on the subsoil, the foundations for brick walls must begin at 2 ft (60 cm) below the surface to prevent the construction breaking up as a result of frost. When it is a matter of, say, four steps, each about 6 in (15 cm) high, more than half the construction (and the cost of it) is buried under ground. Many owners of gardens resent this and therefore seek less expensive solutions.

Sleepers still provide a possible solution and there is in itself nothing to be said against these timbers, which are 6 in (15 cm) thick, 10 in (25 cm) wide and usually 8 ft 4 in (250 cm) long. They are dark, a fair size and neutral in appearance. They look much better, in my opinion, than the dyke-protection posts often employed in the Netherlands nowadays. The fact that the use of sleepers reached saturation point stems from their inappropriate use. Sturdy material demands sturdy planting, and that was often lacking. If they are combined with ivy, tall evergreen ferns and box balls, there is nothing at all wrong with using sleepers, as may be seen in Ankie Dekker's famous modern garden in Veere (Netherlands). She used sleepers to construct the steps leading from the terrace to the garden, and nobody has ever suggested that they are inappropriate there.

Wooden planks

If the requirement is for something natural, it is also possible to use wooden planks for the risers of a flight of steps. Hardwood posts, or ones treated with preservative, are hammered into position to the left and right of the steps, and a plank of the same material is then nailed to them. A flight of steps can be constructed quite simply and inexpensively in this way, and many people consider that it looks much better than sleepers. If the planks are painted dark green or black, or left to turn grey, it is undoubtedly a good solution. They can be backed by clinker bricks, gravel or anything else used to form the tread.

Stone

Anyone who takes the trouble to look round the premises of collectors of old building materials may find blue stone treads and edgings there. For constructions in the vicinity of old buildings, blue stone is undoubtedly a unique material. Sometimes it may be possible to find finished steps specially cut for the purpose and with finely modelled nosing in front. Otherwise, it would be possible to have them recut and

In Mrs Merton's garden at the Old Rectory near Burghfield, glazed clinker bricks have been used for the steps and paths. An irregular bond has been used for the paving between the delicate borders, while the large leaves of the Acanthus mollis *counteract any suggestion of severity.*

A   entrance to garden
B   office
C   terrace constructed of grey stone slabs
    in the sunken garden
D   small pond with stone surround and
    water spout
E   clinker bricks
F   a 6³/₄-in (17-cm) high step extends
    across the entire width of the garden
G   the second step is the same height, thus
    making a total of 13¹/₂ in (34 cm) plus
    the terrace by the house
H   perennials and roses in shades of pink,
    blue, white and lemon yellow
I   summer-house
J   water basin against the brick wall, with
    spouts set in the wall
K   new brick wall
L   pergola with roses

When I arrived at the house of the restoration contractor Oosterhout and his wife in
Wychen (Netherlands), there was a landscaped shrubbery with some tall trees.
Everything meandered and curved. They
were tired of it all and I decided to clear
everything. Not a tree, shrub or hedge was
left standing. Making use of different levels,
I created a spacious garden which begins
with a small sunken pond, continues with a
fair-sized lawn and ends with a large one.
Beyond that, there is what I consider an
attractive summer-house flanked by water
basins bricked into the wall and spouts producing a tinkling sound. All this is enclosed
within a wealth of perennials and roses in
shades of pinkish purple and blue.
Two pergolas give the 'sun-and-shade' terrace a sense of intimacy, and a new brick
wall has been built all round the garden.
A finished complex, just what was wanted
by the client, who carried out the work to
perfection.

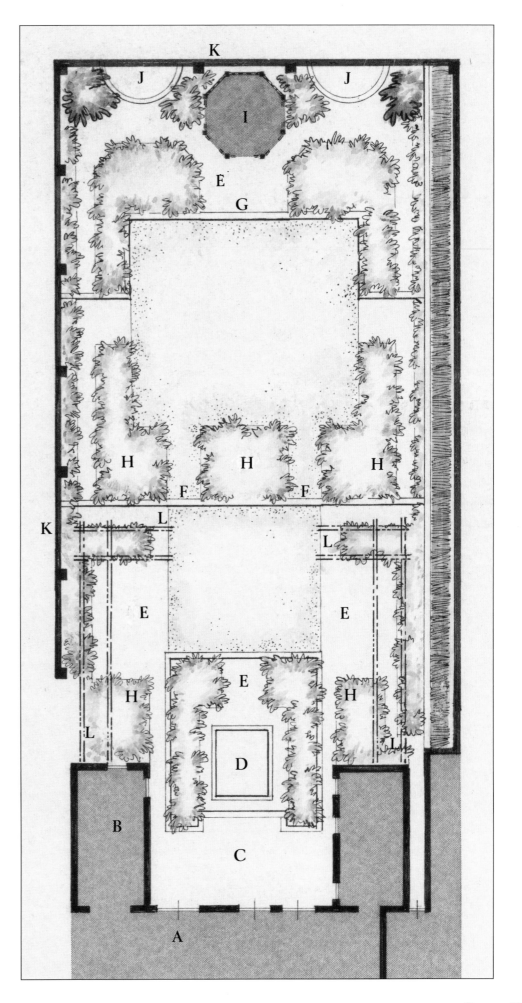

Chatsworth House near Bakewell in Derbyshire is the home of the Dukes of Devonshire. This maze forms part of a powerful interplay of granite blocks, hedges and flights of steps, and a few free-growing plant forms to relieve the rigidity. Oblique light can thus create theatrical effects which change by the hour.

copied from original models to achieve a handsome effect near an old building. If modelled treads are neither required nor easily found, there are also simple straight stone slabs which are even used for modern buildings.

Concrete

Anyone wishing to construct a really inexpensive flight of steps can do so by placing large concrete slabs measuring 20 in x 20 in (50 cm x 50 cm) upright in the ground, leaving 6 in (15 cm) projecting. Horizontal slabs of the same size are then placed on top over an infill of sand, possibly mixed with some cement to hold it in place. Simple neutral steps can be constructed quite easily in this way.

Weser sandstone

As an alternative to the materials already mentioned, Weser sandstone can also be used for making steps. Paving stones made from this material are called flagstones. It varies from reddish brown to slightly sand-coloured, difficult shades which go very well with modern architecture. Large slabs of this material were used at Walenburg Castle and many large houses built in the Netherlands at the beginning of the twentieth century.

The material is also satisfactory for making steps. There are long stone slabs which can be used for this, often with a flagstone as a tread on top. In England as well as in the Netherlands, however, it is more usual to find a combination of brick risers and treads, with flagstones used as stiffeners between them and with them.

Wooden decks

A terrace and adjoining steps made of timber planking go very well with modern white houses, and even with older houses furnished in a modern style. These large wooden steps and decks are successfully constructed in many places nowadays. Sometimes there is a construction of railway sleepers on which the planks are laid; elsewhere there may be a framework of posts and beams to which the planks are attached.

It is possible to choose greying hardwood of the kind approved by environmental organizations. Fortunately, there is also treated softwood from the Scandinavian commercial forests, which should last for at least fifteen years. It makes sense to enquire about any guarantees for the product, since replacements are expensive enough anyway! People who do not like greyish colours can stain their decks black. Floor stain works very well on softwood, but less so on hardwood as there are few or only very small pores into which the stain can penetrate.

Tim Vaughan designed this garden for Yvon Serge in Brittany. There the houses and roofs are grey which, as is apparent here, can be sophisticated rather than boring. Variations in the colour of the paving suddenly turn out to be superfluous, provided green shapes add tranquillity and light-heartedness.

Terraces

There are few areas which are so easy to arrange symmetrically as a terrace. A single seat with a statue, a column, a tree or an identical number of pots on each side is all that is needed to achieve a symmetrical scheme. It is always possible, of course, to go much further, as can be seen from the many examples created in various countries.

Starting with a seat

The Lutyens seat, named after the famous English architect who often collaborated with Gertrude Jekyll, is an attractive piece of furniture for forming the focal point of a symmetrical arrangement. The Chinese influences incorporated in this seat are unique and quite inimitable. The curves to the back are imaginative and go well with the loose forms of plants. Cane or hardwood chairs can be placed near it, as well as a fanciful round table or a rectangular hardwood one. People are unlikely to have two of these seats on a terrace, although, from a decorative point of view, they might look very good on either side of the garden door. Rather a severe shape is obviously required for a terrace, though severity should not be taken too far. Cast-iron seats, usually with a light framework and seats and backs each consisting of two parts, are classics. They should be combined with bistro-type chairs, again with a cast-iron framework and slatted backs and seats. A stone table with iron legs fits in best with such seating. An interesting effect is achieved if the entire framework is painted dark green and the tabletop, made of Namur blue stone, varies from dark to light grey. A cast-iron table in bistro-style can of course be added as well. The straight backs of the seat and chairs make these items highly suitable for meals out of doors.

For lazing purposes there is the old-fashioned slatted seat: a cast-iron framework transformed by a large number of horizontal slats into a low seat with a slightly curved back. This makes it very comfortable for relaxing and enjoying the sunshine. Comfortable cane chairs such as the well-known Lloyd Loom chairs go well with this. There are, however, many other kinds of cane chairs which can be left out of doors all through the summer and need not be taken inside until autumn.

In addition to all these somewhat nostalgic types, there are also modern seats such as the Erlau seat which looked so striking at the 1992 Floriade at Zoetermeer in the Netherlands. This is a modern

Photograph on pages 118/119: *Two artists, Paula Thies and Jaap Nieuwenhuis, live in a house by the River IJssel in the Netherlands, where they have created a box and yew topiary garden. The terrace is somewhat obscured by this medley of green forms.*

Above: *The shutters are black and the garden furniture is painted mauvish blue at Jaap Nieuwenhuis' house.*

Far right, below: *In the Dutch province of North Brabant, door and window frames were often painted yellow ochre. A new harmony is created if that colour is reflected in the garden furniture. Joop Braam has achieved that effect here in Dongen.*

version of the slatted seat: a galvanized aluminium sheet was pressed into the correct shape and provided with feet to create a superlight and extremely comfortable seat which looks smart too. It is not so easy though to choose the right chairs to go with it, but the various pavement café chairs made of iron tubing with cane or synthetic wire seats are quite suitable in any case.

Those who like a Spartan look will enjoy the modern concrete seats with their extended U-shape. This 'evergreen' consists of a long seat with sides cast onto it. Slats are available to put on the actual seat and prevent people getting cold. There are U-block chairs to go with it: 16 x 16 x 16-in (40 x 40 x 40-cm) concrete U-shapes with or without slatted seats. Seat and chairs fit in well with modern houses where 'false' romanticism would be inappropriate.

It is obvious that all these arrangements can be symmetrical, even if it is decided to have a table with a seat at each of the long sides and a chair at each end.

If the seat is low, it is best to have a low table as well, though it need not be placed right in front of the seat. People want to move about out of doors, and obstacles may be annoying. A table in the

corner between two seats placed at right angles to each other would then be an ideal arrangement.

One type of seat still needs mentioning, although it is more suitable for public gardens or a terrace belonging to a modern house. This type is made of wire and is shaped like a slatted seat. The individual units can be linked together to form a circle, and look very attractive in several areas of the old Flemish city of Bruges. The material is comfortable to sit on provided one is wearing thick clothing to protect one's back and posterior. The construction is open and graceful, especially if the seats can be linked together to form a semicircle, or if they are arranged round a tree.

Stone seats and chairs

Because people want to be able to move seats and chairs around easily these days, light items are preferred. Stone is obviously heavy and no longer used much for garden furniture. Only tables are still made of stone, sometimes with pedestal feet, and sometimes with a wooden framework. Seats made of stone, marble, granite or sandstone

Architecture may consist of hedges, buildings and... swimming pools. Here at the Manoir d'Eyrignac in the Dordogne, these features were combined to create a sober effect.

were very popular in ancient gardens. They required very little maintenance and were scarcely affected by the weather. In formal gardens, they were specially arranged so as to form architectural features that underlined the overall design. In large parks such seats were backless; in private gardens they usually had backs. Magnificent examples have been preserved since, like steps, fountains and summer-houses, they were made of costly material.

Unfortunately, it has become almost prohibitively expensive to have new blue stone seats made. Round or rectangular sandstone seats constitute a modern and more affordable alternative. There should be a fixed table to go with them. Such an arrangement can fit in very well with a terrace in the same colour, a few garden walls in the same material, or a house in the same colour. One major advantage of such items of furniture is that they are indestructible. They look inviting in places where they are not visible from the house, but where an area for sitting and eating is required. They are often installed by swimming pools, in woods, by marshy areas or ponds.

The terrace as part of the symmetrical plan of the house

A symmetrical plan and elevations with regular door and window patterns constituted the ideal type of design for domestic buildings that was favoured by architects and clients alike for many centuries. A symmetrical staircase and a symmetrical terrace obviously formed part of such a scheme. The serenity and apparent naturalness of this type of building is still to be seen in many older-type houses. Even in the heyday of the English landscape style, the terrace still formed part of the symmetrical plan of the house, whereas all was asymmetrical beyond it.

Influenced by the English rural architectural style, however, even terraces adjoining the house became asymmetrical in the late nineteenth and early twentieth centuries. Flagstones, clinker bricks or tiles were used to pave such terraces, which were often constructed in a recess at the back of the house. Part of the house – the dining room, for instance – often projected beyond the main elevation, and the terrace, usually facing south, was built in the re-entrant that had thus been created. Symmetry, however, can still be introduced in this kind of

The long lines of the deck guide the eye towards the distant view. The wood featured in Hannah Peschar's garden is therefore a place to create a world of one's own close to and yet remote from everything. Hannah's occupation as a gallery owner constitutes the leitmotiv *in this large garden. (Designed by Anthony Paul.)*

A spacious long hall with door leading to garden
B grey, 16 x 24 in (40 x 60 cm) concrete tiles; terrace with a dining table, a large Italian umbrella and lots of pots
C shady terrace with a Lutyens seat and pots
D tall yew hedge
E two tall conifer columns
F two lilacs
G two grey-leafed ornamental pear trees (Pyrus salicifolia) and plenty of bamboo
H rhythm of Osmarea clipped into rounded shape
I border: white Phlox and Stachys olympica
J white-flowered perennials with box edgings and yew pyramids in the centres
K grass path and small lawns
L to amber-coloured garden
M to swimming-pool garden enclosed within hedges and cut off from view

The garden was narrowest just where a grandiose effect was required at the end of the spacious hall with windows extending down to floor level. I therefore decided to create the effect of depth with the rows of box, and the effect of space with white-flowered plants. The yew topi-ary was added later to create a more dramatic effect. The Lutyens seat, with the hedge and pointed or rounded forms of shrubs and conifers behind and around it, makes a handsome focal point. A lot of bamboo was planted to the left and right to provide evergreen luxury. The terrace became a large one for groups of friends and visitors. Wicker chairs are surrounded by a large number of box spirals, and a large umbrella provides shade for gateaus and summer salads. Another area of this garden is shown in the plan on page 45 – the White Garden is to the rear, and the Blue Garden is in front.

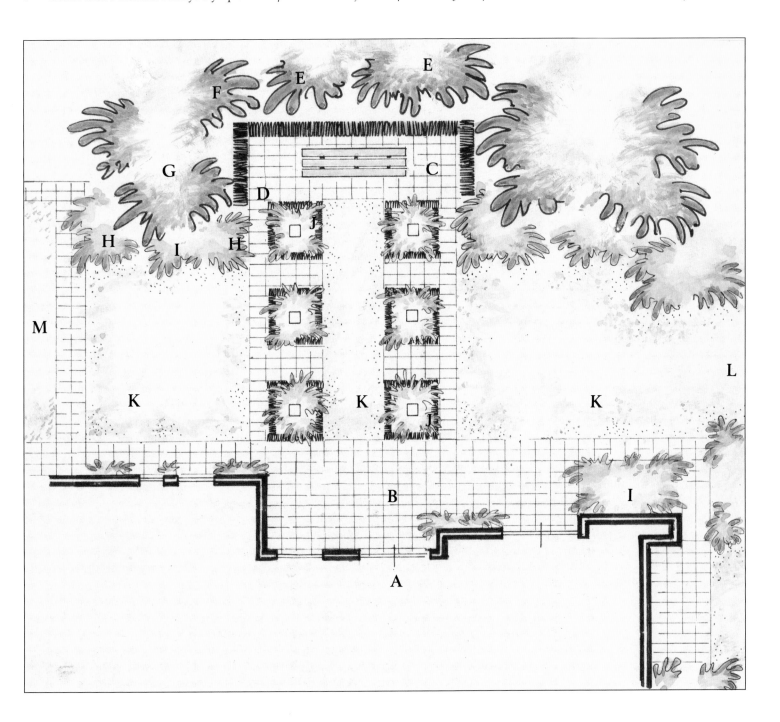

The atmosphere, layout and planting of
Mr and Mrs Ingram's private garden at
Garsington Manor in Oxfordshire are
Italian. Vivid colours prevail in the spacious
flower beds, here filled with tulips, while delicate restrained shades have been chosen for
the terraces, summer-house and terrace
planting. The effect is refined Tuscan rather
than extravagantly southern.

asymmetrical sitting area. A greying hardwood seat against a wall or under a window, with a table and a couple of chairs in front of it, is an arrangement which may be seen in many places. A few pots and an umbrella are all that is needed to create an ideal spot for relaxing.

There has been a tendency in recent years to restore the ancient symmetrical architectural forms. Post-Modernism uses classical forms capriciously – and sometimes abuses them. Symmetrically furnished terraces and flights of steps are part of the trend.

The terrace freely placed in the garden

Walda Pairon has her ornamental pleasure garden – called Giardini – at Kalmthout near Antwerp. The round areas paved with clinker bricks present a constantly changing scene with pots, statuary and plants.

In many designs for gardens, certainly in the more or less formal examples, terraces are constructed somewhere in the garden to terminate the visual axis from the house. A seat serving as a focal point on such a terrace is an ideal object for making the tension between the house and the garden both visible and palpable.

Depending on the style of the house, it would be possible to choose a modest greying English park seat with pots of busy Lizzies beside it, or else a more dramatically designed seat with more exotic plants. A monumental white garden seat fits in well with a large old-fashioned house with a lot of white window-sills, while a black-stained seat will look well with a modern house. Dark green is always a good colour for a seat because it is such an inconspicuous shade in a garden.

A separate terrace for such a sitting area somewhere in the garden is highly convenient as the garden furniture does not then always need to be put away. A composition of seating elements with a few pots, a bird bath and perhaps even a statue will be created almost without effort.

A dwarf wall, usually about 16 in (40 cm) high, creates a practical and attractive finish to a terrace, and can be used as a seat. Where the house is built of brick, the wall should be constructed with bricks of the same colour. If the house is plastered, the wall should be treated in the same way. Concrete is another suitable material for a dwarf wall. An arrangement of cushions or slats on top of the wall is an attractive and practical way of adding to its comfort. It is advisable to make concrete walls so massive that a heavy visual line is formed. A lot of foliage plants behind the wall help to create a strong garden feature.

This type of wall can also be used to stand pots on and, combined with, say, a sculpture, this can create an attractive arrangement.

The covered terrace as a symmetrical focal point

The 'covered seat' – a seat with a rear wall, a zinc roof and sides of trellis painted green – comes from America. For some reason, these seats are still relatively unknown in Britain although, in such a wet climate, there could well be a need for a dry place to sit under a lean-to roof.

Subtle differences in colour create a sense of space.
The clinker bricks in the foreground are set in mortar unlike those in the long strip, which makes the latter look slightly greenish. The gravel has a golden colour and the terra-cotta pots are reddish.

In this part of the garden at the Lower Hall in Worfield, Shropshire, the pergolas have brought about a complete integration between the house, the garden and the terrace. Shrubs have been planted against the house, thus blending the colours of wall and terrace.
(Source: Gardens of England and Wales, 1994 ed.)

Far left: *At Jabbeke in Belgium, Yolande Van de Maele has decorated her large, simple blue stone terrace with hard materials. Iron, glass and tin repeat the shades of grey, thus creating a new entity.*

Erwan Tymen designed this garden for Monsieur and Madame Peché who live in Brittany. Moss is allowed to grow in the joints between the blue stone terrace. The pots contain large-leafed plants including Gunnera, *a native of Brazil, which can survive very well in them.*

It is more usual in Britain to create a dry place to sit by constructing some kind of a pergola with wire, wooden posts or other material. With creepers, wistaria or roses growing over it, this obviously looks an attractive, if not always a totally rainproof solution.

A barbecue can be bricked into a dry sitting area, and a pond in front of its adds some drama to the view.

Two sitting areas, to the left and right of the line of vision

If a pond, or a statue, or a hedge made of handsome plants forms a focal point at the end of the line of vision within a symmetrical layout, it is obviously impossible to create a sitting area in a central position. It would, however, be possible to have terraces used as sitting areas to the left and right of the line of vision. The garden owner will discover that this need not be boring but is in fact quite practical, since it often provides a choice between sitting in the sun or in the shade. The arrangement of the terraces need not actually be symmetrical as well. Symmetry, after all, must never be stifling but should inspire people to think of new ideas and solutions.

Architectural Features

Summer-houses

There are many ways of including architectural features in a symmetrical layout. A striking example is a beautiful lattice-work summer-house in the centre of an evenly divided rose garden. This kind of architectural jewel in the centre is something that can be admired in many gardens. The most celebrated example is undoubtedly the rose summer-house in the White Garden at Sissinghurst Castle, where iron arches form a dome overgrown with white-flowered roses.

Something similar is also to be seen in the lovely rose garden of Tyninghame House in East Lothian, not far from Edinburgh. Here, the owner copied the model of a baroque tea-house, but without a roof. Lady Haddington, an American by birth who married a Scottish earl and owner of several fine castles, brought this familiar American type of summer-house with her to Scotland. Lattice-work summer-houses are practical in their country of origin since they form windbreaks without keeping out the wind entirely. This is essential in the hotter southern States, where shelter from the heat of the sun is sought under trees or in lattice-work summer-houses with closed roofs. That is not the case at Tyninghame: there is hardly ever too much sunshine... and the roses themselves will provide enough shade as soon as they have grown through the trellis roof.

This Scottish summer-house, frequently copied by other garden owners, is painted or stained a pale shade of lavender blue.

Wells

The rose arches at Sissinghurst Castle and the wooden lattice-work summer-house at Tyninghame House are just two examples of the many ways of creating an architectural central feature in a section of the garden.

There is, for example, the well, a functional feature found even in the oldest gardens. Monastic and castle gardens are almost unthinkable without one or more of these useful central features. A wooden or iron construction was usually fitted above the well's stone or brick superstructure, and a bucket on a rope would be suspended from it. Wellheads of this type are functional, but we often find them turned into graceful masterpieces of wrought-ironwork, especially in southern countries. They might appear rather over-decorated further north. Even so, a stone or brick wellhead with an iron superstructure can look

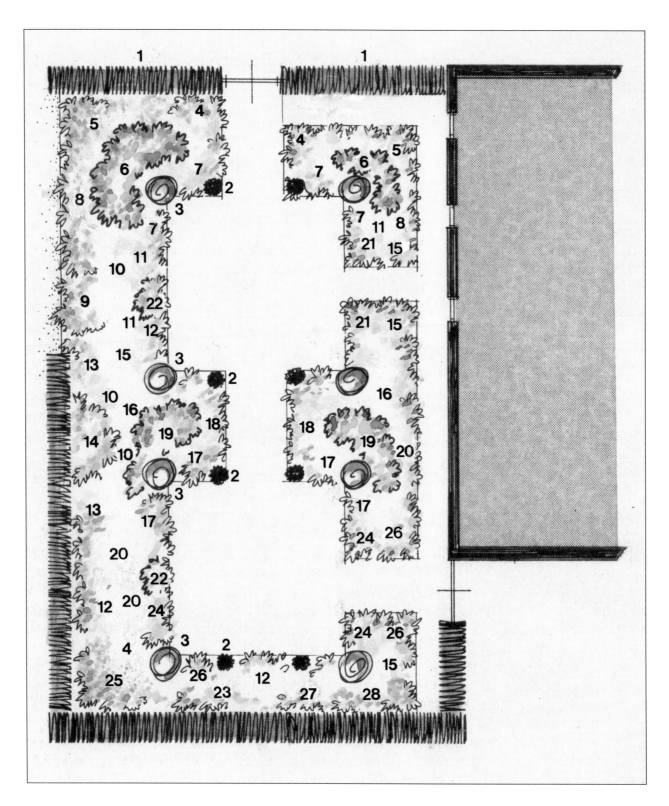

The yellow and orange flower garden (Q) from page 30.

1   Fagus sylvatica, *hedge*
2   *box balls*
3   Skimmia formanii
4   Lysimachia ephemerum
5   Aconitum *'Spark's Var.'*
6   Rosa *'Golden Wings'*
7   Lavandula *'Hidcote Var.'*
8   Anchusa *'Dropmore Scarlet'*

9   Delphinium *'Andenken an August Koenemann'*
10 Aconitum napellus
11 Alstroemeria *'Orange King'*
12 Aster alpinus
13 Anemone *'Honorine Jobert'*
14 Delphinium *'Völkerfrieden'*
15 Solidago *'Laurin'*
16 Astrantia maxima *'Rosea'*
17 Azalea mollis *'Harvest Moon'*
18 Campanula portenschlagiana

19 Rosa *'Lady of the Dawn'*
20 Aster novi-belgii *'Little Boy Blue'*
21 Buphtalmum salicifolium
22 Syringa meyeri *'Palibin'*
23 Delphinium moerheimii
24 Gypsophila *'Rosenschleier'*
25 Helenium hoopesii
26 Centaurea dealbata
27 Campanula lactiflora *'Loddon Anna'*
28 Delphinium *'King Arthur'*

quite pleasing if it has good planting and either brick or stone paving round it.

Severely clipped box topiary, flat or rounded, looks very interesting near a well. If that is considered too stiff, it is always possible to opt for romanticism and surround the well with climbing roses, paving round its edge, a path and lots of herbs, perennials or more roses.

Materials for wells:
clinker brick or stone

In Limburg, in the south of the Netherlands, stone wells are quite common – the material for them is found in their immediate vicinity. In other parts of the Netherlands, the well shafts and wellheads are usually faced with clinker bricks.

A circular stone or brick well still makes a very attractive feature in a herb garden. To create an ornamental wellhead, clinker bricks should be set in mortar round the part of a concrete sewage pipe that projects above ground. It looks best to make such a surround at least two bricks in width, so that enough space is created for pots and seating.

Ornamental wells are usually provided with a concrete bottom these days. An advantage of this is that the water level can be controlled and water can come right up to the top. Any equipment can be camouflaged by a suitably painted lid to the well. With a few roses growing over the well or an old elder, this kind of feature soon becomes part of the garden.

Handsome stone models of wellheads are on sale in many parts of the Netherlands. They are usually round because the excavated shaft was this shape, although there are also square, hexagonal, octagonal and even rectangular wells.

A comparatively plain and preferably smooth wellhead is appropriate for a central position in the garden of a modest house, whereas sculptured and richly decorated wellheads can be interesting in the grounds of grand historic mansions.

If you install a well in a central position in the garden, do not forget to pave the area round it and a path leading up to it.

Small gardens belonging to modest houses do not need to make grandiose gestures but should be delicate and varied. Something of everything was wanted for this one. Note the drinking trough with its inconspicuous planting. The paving material is gravel, with plants unobtrusively spilling over it. (Private garden in Hampshire.)

Photograph on pages 130/131: The garden of Barrington Court in Somerset was designed by Gertrude Jekyll. It has a number of walls that formerly separated kitchen gardens, courtyards and stables from one another. Now everything has become garden, and the vistas, walls and gateways form delightful dividers between gardens with different atmospheres. The simple but beautiful gate creates rhythm and refinement.

Far left: *A gate need not always be high. If it is intended solely for keeping out dogs, geese and toddlers, a low gate may be quite adequate.*
(Fairfield House, Hampshire.)

Left: *A glorious renaissance garden full of colour, mosaics, grass, paths and walls of green stone has been brought to life at Pitmedden Gardens in Scotland. The yew hedges have been clipped imaginatively to form walls resembling theatre boxes.*

Below: *In this private garden in Oxfordshire, the mauvish blue arbour forms a break in the rose garden. The mature standard fruit trees form a green roof which makes the arbour look even more graceful.*

Fountains

The delights of fountains have been dealt with extensively in the chapter on water in the symmetrical garden. A fountain is another feature that should be adapted to the architecture of the house and to its surroundings. Simple fountains are always fascinating, whereas excessively ornate examples are usually a sign of poor taste. Yet even that kind of fountain can be integrated in its surroundings and its dominating impact softened by a lot of planting in its vicinity. Plant small trees all round it so that the fountain is in the shade. You can train *Rosa* 'Albertina' over statues that are overly conspicuous, and make *Clematis* 'Montana' tumble round their feet to create an overgrown and romantic ornamental feature which will always have some charm.

The oldest herbaceous border that I know of is at Arley Hall in Cheshire, south-east of Warrington. There are stone walls on the right; on the left there is a yew hedge. Yew hedges have also been clipped to form side wings and act as an introduction to the wide summer-house where a large family can drink tea and enjoy the interplay of colours.

Right: *Jean Mus created this observation post in Provence. Pots standing on columns line the steps. The apricot shade of the walls is repeated in the climbing roses, and the cypresses add perspective to the view.*

Walls, trellis and niches

Walls are amongst the oldest aids to a systematic subdivision of space. The required effects could be achieved by the creation of square, rectangular, round or oval areas. A long rectangular space could easily be accented at one end by a statue or a niche with a water basin or an open hearth. In a square, it was possible to have a door, a statue niche, or a couple of columns in the centre of each side to create symmetry and yet achieve a kind of tension. A round or oval space seems to demand an accent in the centre.

Translated in terms of a garden 'room', this means that doors, gateways, niches, statuary or fountains can all be used to emphasize symmetry.

Stone walls can obviously be replaced by hedges, and trellis is used for similar purposes in gardens. If one wishes to close off an area from intruders but still wants to enjoy a view and benefit from a breeze, lattice-work constructions can be built all round. In warm climates lattice-work or trellis is therefore used for a great many purposes, whereas in the northerly regions of Europe it is regarded more specifically as a decorative feature. People fit trellis to a wall, behind a seat, in a rose garden, and enjoy the interplay of lines.

All kinds of lattice-work construction are ideal for creating symmetrical focal points in the centre or at the end of a space. They are

*A simple lattice-work construction and a
large pot of glazed earthenware make a handsome focal point against the wall enclosing
this private garden near Fontainebleau.*

At Jenkyn Place in Hampshire, steps and clipped yew hedges constitute powerful architectonic forms. To counteract their severity, pots and an elegant wrought-iron gate have been added to the stage set.

Anyone familiar with the richness of Heale House in Wiltshire and its impressive gardens will realize that the photographer discovered a delightful 'blemish' here. Yet this casual approach touches us more than the costliest gate with gilded ironwork.

In English gardens, people are bold enough to play with blue as a suitable colour for doors, gates and seats. The fact that such boldness is rewarded is apparent in these stable buildings in a private garden in Oxfordshire, where even the clock became a splendid focal point as a result of devoting attention to it and choosing the right colours.

easy to fix at the right level and also open, thus allowing effects of depth to be created.

Closed or half-open structures in the garden: summer-houses and arbours

In many Dutch cities, but particularly in Amsterdam, it is customary to build a closed summer-house at the end of an oblong garden belonging to one of the larger seventeenth-century canalside houses. Such a building forms an ideal, visually attractive, and at the same time practical focal point at the back of the garden.

These summer-houses are usually closed, one-storey structures at ground level, though there are actually some three-storey versions in Amsterdam. People can have meals there in fine weather, and in winter they provide convenient storage space for garden furniture, statuary and non-hardy pot plants. In some instances, the summer-houses have been converted for use as living accommodation.

Summer-houses are often open in hot climates but usually closed in colder regions. They come in all kinds of shapes and sizes. There are

very handsome examples in Portugal, where they are sometimes decorated with tile tableaux. In Italy, the plastered walls are often covered with frescoes, whereas the walls of summer-houses in Britain and France are usually plastered but not painted.

At Hidcote Manor, there are two small and most elegant summer-houses to the left and right of the grass path between two red borders. The soffit of a tiled roof is embellished with Dutch wall tiles. Zinc is sometimes used as a roofing material, particularly along the River Vecht in the Netherlands. Thatch is also used frequently for summer-houses in the same region. Thatched roofs are also common in England for cottages as well as summer-houses.

Anyone wishing to construct a summer-house now will need to bear in mind a number of basic principles. If the summer-house and main house are not far apart, it is almost essential to reproduce some of the lines of the house and to use some similar materials in order to create a measure of uniformity. If the house is red brick, the summer-house should be constructed of the same material. The same roofing material should be used for both the house and the summer-house.

If that seems too monotonous, it would be possible to choose wood for the walls, and roof the house and summer-house with the

Walenburg Castle, where Teus Mandersloot, the full-time gardener, and I have been trying to preserve old-world romanticism for many years. De Nederlandse Tuinenstichting (the Dutch Garden Foundation) funds the preservation of the fragile thing that such a garden proves to be. The combination of plants and topiary is its principal feature.

The columns in the Powis Castle orangery and an equally vertical Rosa 'Gloire de Dijon' *have blended to form a romantic entity.*

Everyone can make use of ornaments and plants to enjoy imaginative symmetry, as illustrated here in the flower garden of Lower Hall.
Glance through the pages of this book again; choose what you admire and adapt it according to the size of your bank balance, the size of your garden and the type of climate you enjoy or suffer. We will be along with pens and cameras...

same material. The reverse is also feasible: similar walls for house and summer-house, but a thatched roof for the summer-house whereas the main house is tiled. If, however, the summer-house is in an isolated position and more or less invisible from the house, it could be constructed entirely of wood and even be roofed with shingles. Cast iron, wrought iron or trellis can be used for a pavilion in a central position as such materials are so obviously intended for the garden that no one would compare them with those of the main house.

There are many ugly examples of modern summer-houses and not so many successful ones, so do not decide too quickly and perhaps ask someone with taste to advise on the design. A great deal of ugliness can of course be concealed by abundant planting.

A summer-house is an ideal structure to have at the bottom end of a garden or at the end of a line of vision. The space in front of it can be filled in many different ways.

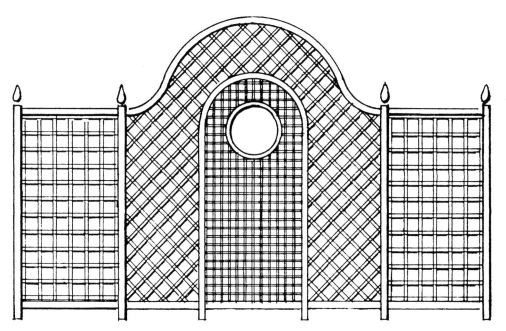

Trellis: Ideal as a symmetrical feature in a central or terminal position.

Index